WITHDRAWN

CONGRESS AND NATIONAL DEFENSE

CONGRESS AND NATIONAL DEFENSE

The Politics of the Unthinkable

Werner J. Feld
John K. Wildgen

PRAEGER

PRAEGER SPECIAL STUDIES • PRAEGER SCIENTIFIC

New York • Philadelphia • Eastbourne, UK
Toronto • Hong Kong • Tokyo • Sydney

Library of Congress Cataloging in Publication Data

Feld, Werner J.
   Congress and national defense

   Includes index.
   1. United States—Military policy. 2. Strategy.
3. United States. Congress. 4. Atomic weapons.
I. Wildgen, John K. II. Title.
UA23.F39 1985 355'.0335'73 84-16007
ISBN 0-03-069751-4 (alk. paper)

Published and Distributed by the
Praeger Publishers Division
(ISBN Prefix 0-275)
of Greenwood Press, Inc.,
Westport, Connecticut

Published in 1985 by Praeger Publishers
CBS Educational and Professional Publishing
a Division of CBS Inc.
521 Fifth Avenue, New York, NY 10175 USA

© 1985 by Praeger Publishers

All rights reserved

56789 052 987654321

Printed in the United States of America
on acid-free paper

PREFACE

There is no shortage of books on either the Congress or strategic thinking. But it is not easy to find the strategic premises behind expressions of defense views in Congress. Part of this is due to the fact that genuinely strategic thinking is as rare in Congress as it is in the general public, even in that segment of the public thought of as attentive to defense and foreign policy concerns.

This book is very much the outcome of a quest for the kind of long-term congressional thinking, as contrasted with pragmatic, day-to-day problem solving, that, as Edward N. Luttwak has argued, is the hallmark of strategy—something alien to Americans. Our purpose here is not to describe or somehow survey disparate congressional views or bloc voting patterns but to isolate those who show signs of truly strategic thinking. It has been our premise that these members of Congress have an influence over their colleagues and the executive that transcends constituency or partisan interests. In some instances, defense planners may follow congressional thinking; in even more cases, they may anticipate reactions from Congress using knowledge of what recognized congressional strategists are thinking. It is the possessors of this kind of intellectual power base whom we pursue in an attempt to discern the thought processes that guide them.

This book tries to make strategic thinking somewhat less alien to its readers, describes the context in which members of Congress find so many pragmatic problems that distract them from long-term thinking, surveys some of the varieties of both strategic and less-than-strategic thinking found in Congress, and then moves on to an examination of where we find the best and most important aspects of strategic thinking: it is concentrated on Europe and on arms control issues.

In preparing this work we had the gracious help of several members of the House and Senate who provided us with documents and background information—some of it fugitive. University of New Orleans librarians, especially Marilyn Hankel, expedited the flow of material to us. Janet Davis typed and typed again numerous drafts. The University of New Orleans Computer Research Center was of material assistance in the preparation of our figures. Finally, we wish to thank our colleagues at the University of New Orleans and the University of Innsbruck for their support, patience, and their sometimes heated but always generous dissent from our approach and views.

Werner J. Feld   John K. Wildgen

New Orleans, July 1984

GLOSSARY

ABM	antiballistic missile
ABRV	advanced ballistic reentry vehicle
ALCM	air launched cruise missile
ASAT	antisatellite
AWACS	airborne warning and control system
CMB	confidence-building measure
CND	campaign for nuclear disarmament
CODA	Congressional Office of Defense Appraisal (proposed)
CRS	Congressional Research Service
CSCE	Conference on Security and Cooperation in Europe
DOD	Department of Defense
EMT	equivalent megatonnage
ERW	Enhanced Radiation Weapon (neutron bomb)
GLCM	ground-launched cruise missile
ICBM	intercontinental ballistic missile (land-based)
INF	intermediate range nuclear forces
MAD	mutual assured destruction
MBFR	mutual and balanced force reductions
MIRV	multiple independently targeted reentry vehicle
NATO	North Atlantic Treaty Organization
NEACP	National Emergency Airborne Command Pose (US)
RV	reentry vehicle
SAC	Strategic Air Command (US)
SALT	Strategic Arms Limitation Treaty/Talks
SLBM	sea-launched ballistic missiles
SSKP	single-shop kill probability
START	Strategic Arms Reduction Talks
WTO	Warsaw Treaty Organization

CONTENTS

Preface	v
Glossary	vii
List of Tables	xi
List of Figures	xiii

1. **EAST-WEST RELATIONS: A SURVEY OF MIXED SIGNALS** — 1
   - The Balance of Terror: Differing Perceptions — 3
   - East-West Solutions — 19
   - The Nuclear Dilemma and East-West Accomodations — 23
   - The U.S. Military: Interests and Management Performance — 26
   - Notes — 28

2. **CONGRESSIONAL ORGANIZATION AND PROCESS REGARDING DEFENSE ISSUES** — 31
   - Organizational Aspects — 34
   - The Policy Making Process — 37
   - Notes — 47

3. **MAJOR CONGRESSIONAL VIEWS ON STRATEGIC WEAPONS SYSTEMS: THE UNTHINKABLE CONGRESS MUST PONDER** — 49
   - Imposing Order on Chaos — 49
   - Reagan's Strategic Map — 50
   - The Rationale behind the Shopping List — 51
   - Some Illustrative Congressional Views — 53
   - Strategic Weapons: The Continuing Debate over the MX — 61
   - Conclusion — 72
   - Notes — 74

4. **WARFARE IN THE EUROPEAN THEATER: DIVIDED OPINIONS IN CONGRESS** — 77
   - NATO Enters the Mid-80s — 77
   - NATO and the Warsaw Pact — 78
   - Notes — 93

5.	**NUCLEAR WEAPONS FREEZE AND ARMS CONTROL**	95
	Freeze and Peace Movements	95
	Congressional Opposition to the Nuclear Freeze	97
	CRS Freeze Approaches	99
	Revival of SALT II?	104
	The Cohen-Nunn Build-Down Proposals	105
	Realistic Prospects for the Build-Down	109
	Notes	111
6.	**WHICH ROAD TO PEACE?**	113
	Notes	118

Index	121
About the Authors	127

LIST OF TABLES

1.1	Comparison of U.S. and Soviet Nuclear Arsenals, 1982	5
1.2	Comparison of WTO and NATO Theater Nuclear Weapons in Europe	14
1.3	Growing Neutralism (1983)	17
1.4	The Attractiveness of NATO (1981)	17
1.5	Confidence in U.S. Global Policy and Reliability as a Military Ally (1982)	18
5.1	Comparison of Major Freeze Proposals	102

LIST OF FIGURES

1.1	Number of Strategic Delivery Vehicles and Warheads (1971-81)	6
1.2	Land-Based ICBM Vulnerability	8
2.1	Defense-related Senate Committees and Sub-committees	35
3.1	Nuclear Budget Breakdown	52
3.2	Total Obligational Authority, History and Projection	55
3.3	Total Obligational Authority, Constant 1984 dollars	56
4.1	Comparisons of NATO and WTO Forces	80
4.2	Comparison of NATO and WTO Total Defense Costs	92

CONGRESS AND NATIONAL DEFENSE

1
EAST-WEST RELATIONS: A SURVEY OF MIXED SIGNALS

In his book *The Europeans*, Luigi Barzini puts forth a "law" that states that "nations, organizations, institutions, bodies, or single human beings are never as powerful, intelligent, far-seeing, efficient, and dangerous as they seem to their enemies."[1] If this proposition is correct (and there appears to be much historical evidence that this is the case), then it spotlights a possibly difficult dilemma in U.S. defense policy formulation. Are we overestimating our "enemy," the Soviet Union? Do the United States and the Soviet Union behave like two armed blind men, as Henry Kissinger wrote, who each believes himself in mortal danger from the other, whom he considers to have perfect foresight, vision, consistency, and coherence in contrast to his own capability?[2] Both superpowers are undoubtedly dangerous, but each is most likely not as dangerous as perceived by its adversary. Indeed, as Kissinger points out, uncertainty, compromise, and incoherence are frequently the essence of policy making.

If, then, our perception of the Soviet Union's real strength might well be blurred, it is reasonable to assume that U.S. defense policy makers are inclined to compensate for the consequent uncertainties by overestimating U.S. security needs and possibly to embark on larger arms programs than may be necessary. Soviet secrecy and inadequate military intelligence encourage this tendency. Contributing to such a trend is the understandable propensity of the military leadership of both superpowers to focus on worst-case scenarios and to highlight the respective "enemy's" actual and potential capabilities.

These circumstances provide the basic context within which defense budget votes are taken in Congress. Naturally, local conditions in each representative's district and each senator's state play a powerful role in how votes are cast by individual members of Congress. Benefits from arms production facilities and military installations for the constituents within districts and states are likely to have a significant influence on the direction of congressional votes. Overarching these considerations are the images members of Congress hold on East-West relations in general, the comparative strengths of the nuclear and conventional arsenals possessed by the two superpowers, and the best strategies to be pursued by the United States for the assurance of U.S. security while at the same time avoiding a nuclear holocaust. The formation and subsequent changes of these images are likely to be materially affected by the views on defense and security matters expressed by a relatively small number of senators and representatives who have gained a reputation of having carefully studied the problems and have become acknowledged experts in their fields. Indeed, the expertise of the members of Congress has been recognized by the executive branch, and their views on particular issues are analyzed, if not accepted.

With U.S. policy makers faced with crucial choices regarding national defense in the 1980s and beyond that will have far-reaching implications not only for the superpowers but for the whole world, it seems to us extremely important to analyze and assess the views and perspectives of the congressional experts on U.S. security and defense. While it is difficult to pinpoint the spread effect of the opinions and to determine their causality for ultimate U.S. policies, roll-call analyses on important votes may provide insights into their influence on senators and representatives. These analyses, as well as the careful examination of their statements in various forums and in print, may help us in making projections for the future formulation of U.S. defense policy. Considering the enormous stakes involved in this area of policy making that might entail U.S. casualties in the tens of millions, the vast destruction of U.S. cities, and complete change in the life we are accustomed to, this volume intends to explore the politics of the unthinkable.

Before proceeding to the assessment of what congressional defense experts think and perceive, we must provide a brief survey of the international political environment. U.S. defense and security policy does not operate in a vacuum; it is not simply a given based on a set of military and economic capabilities. Rather, it reacts to stimuli emanating from both potential enemies and allies. Obviously, it must be able to respond to external military threats, but it must also take into account the needs and views of the U.S. allies. All this requires knowledge and understanding by those who are confronted by budget requests from the military. And this knowledge can often be obtained only with great difficulty because of Soviet secrecy, the aspirations of U.S. allies at times divergent from those of the United States, and the vested interests of the U.S. armed forces. Therefore, what the congressional experts may hear and see are mixed signals from abroad and home, and it is essential that we seek to identify these signals and bring them into some kind of order.

THE BALANCE OF TERROR: DIFFERING PERCEPTIONS
The Meaning of Figures

It is generally accepted that the peace between the United States and the Soviet Union up to now has been maintained by the deterrent effects of the strategic nuclear arsenals of the two superpowers. Strategic weapons are those that can hit Soviet territory from either the United States or submarines or vice versa.

The targets of strategic nuclear weapons can be either military installations, including, most importantly, nuclear launch facilities, or industry directly supporting the war effort or contributing to economic recovery. Another set of targets consists of cities in general and their populations. If retaliation against a first strike is involved, aiming at the first category of targets is known as counterforce retaliation, while taking aim at the second is labeled countervalue retaliation.

The number of strategic missiles in the respective arsenals of the superpowers is pretty well established. The missiles are either land-based (intercontinental ballistic missiles, or ICBMs), submarine-based (sea-launched ballistic missiles, or SLBMs), or carried by long-range bombers. Each missile or bomber may carry more than one warhead. ICBMs and SLBMs equipped with so-called multiple independently targeted reentry vehicles (MIRVs) may have as many as ten warheads. Bombers obviously can carry more than ten nuclear weapons. The number of warheads, however, is not equivalent with the destructive power of these weapons. Rather, destructiveness of weapons is measured in terms of megatons of TNT, or millions of tons of this explosive.

One megaton of explosives equals 1,000 kilotons (kt); the U.S. nuclear bombs dropped on Hiroshima and Nagasaki had an explosive power of about 20 kt. The measurement used at present for destructive power is EMT or equivalent megatonnage.

Finally, another measurement of strategic nuclear power is the payload of the delivery vehicles. This refers to the weight that can be carried by the missile launchers to the targets and includes not only the warheads but also the guidance systems. In terms of payload, the U.S. bomber force provides significant advantages, but, when only ICBMs are compared, the Soviet Union is well ahead.

Table 1.1 provides comparisons of the U.S. and Soviet arsenals. It shows several interesting facets of the nuclear strategic competition. First, although the United States has fewer strategic launchers than the Soviet Union, it has more deliverable warheads. Second, while the Soviet Union has more land- and sea-based launchers, the United States has a greater number of sea- and air-deliverable warheads. Third, the Soviet Union outshines the United States in all measurements with respect to land-based weapons. Fourth, in terms of destructive power, the Soviet Union is almost twice as strong as the United States. Fifth, the greatest U.S. strength lies in its bomber force, and this shows up in all four categories. Without the bombers (B-52s and later B-1s), U.S. nuclear power would be greatly diminished, and yet the employment of this force depends on the aircraft's ability to overcome Moscow's increasingly effective antiaircraft defenses. However, this vulnerability may be overcome as the U.S. bomber force is increasingly equipped with air-launched cruise missiles (ALCMs), which will permit delivery of these very accurate nuclear weapons well outside Soviet territory and far from Soviet air defenses.[3]

While, then, in terms of numbers there is a substantial imbalance between the U.S. and Soviet strategic nuclear arsenals that clearly favors Moscow, it is important to note that the Soviet buildup began after Moscow's embarrassment in the Cuban missile crisis in 1962, has continued vigorously until today, and shows no slackening in the early 1980s. The trends in strategic delivery vehicles and warheads from 1971 to 1981 can be seen in figure 1.1, which includes British strategic nuclear forces. The existing U.S. disadvantages would be eliminated after 1985 when deployment of the ALCM and Trident II, which already has begun, is complete and when the MX ICBM becomes operational in 1986,[4] if Congress approves its funding.

Does the current imbalance in the strategic nuclear arsenals mean that the principle of deterrence involving mutual assured destruction

Table 1.1. Comparison of U.S. and Soviet Nuclear Arsenals, 1982

	Strategic Launchers U.S.	Strategic Launchers USSR	Deliverable Nuclear Warheads U.S.	Deliverable Nuclear Warheads USSR	Destructive Power (EMT) U.S.	Destructive Power (EMT) USSR	Payload (1,000 lbs.) U.S.	Payload (1,000 lbs.) USSR
ICBMs	1,050	1,398	2,150	5,900	1,400	4,900	2,450	10,025
SLBMs	554	920	5,000	1,600	825	1,150	1,700	2,175
Bombers	375	150	2,700	300	1,650	300	23,500	5,100
	1,969	2,468	9,900	7,800	3,875	6,350	27,650	17,300

Source: Adapted from Albert Carnesale et al. (the Harvard Nuclear Study Group), *Living With Nuclear Weapons* (New York: Bantam Books, 1983), p. 120.

Figure 1.1. Number of Strategic Delivery Vehicles and Warheads (1971-81).

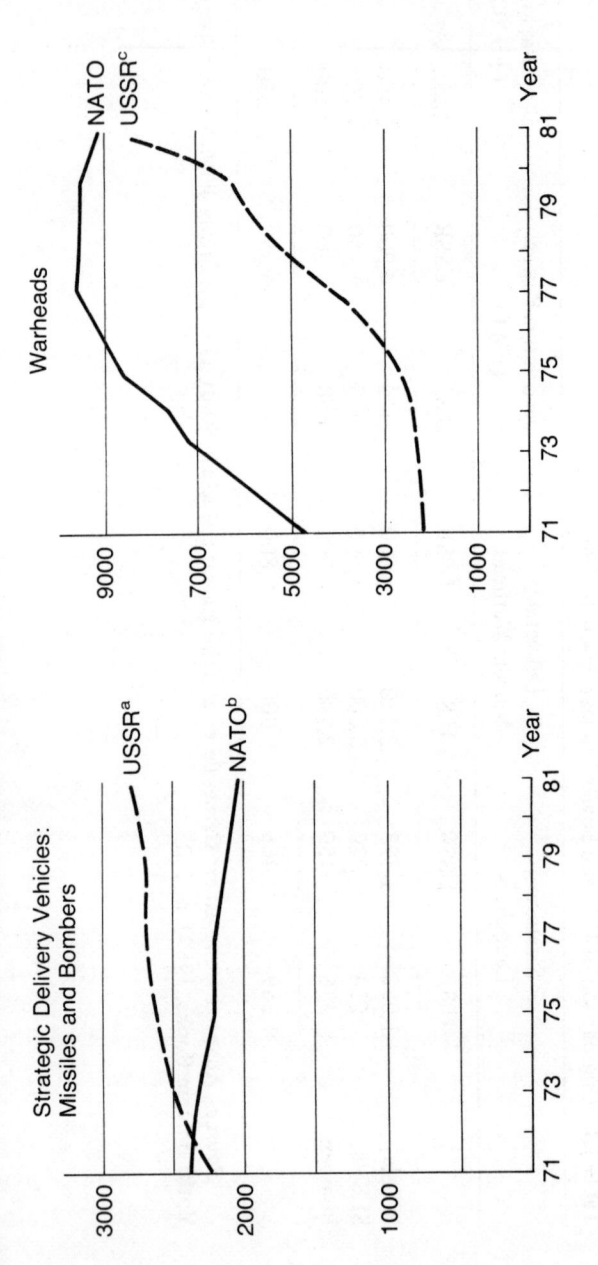

[a]USSR figures include Soviet strategic missiles and BEAR, BISON, and BACKFIRE bombers; the BACKFIRE bomber has been included in this figure because it has an inherent intercontinental capability although in its maritime and European land-attack roles it poses a serious threat to NATO Europe.

[b]NATO figures include United States strategic missiles, 64 British strategic POLARIS SLBMs and United States B-52s and FB-111s. The United States-based FB-111 is included because it has a strategic mission.

[c]If all USSR missiles were MIRVed to their tested capability, the number of Soviet warheads would total some 8,500.

Source: NATO and the Warsaw Pact—Force Comparisons, (Brussels: NATO, 1982), pp. 39, 40.

(MAD) in the event of either superpower initiating a nuclear exchange is no longer valid? This is a key question, and on its answer depends the judgment as to how far the modernization and expansion of the U.S. nuclear arsenal is to be funded. Several considerations appear to be relevant in this connection. First, the destructive power of nuclear weapons must be counterpoised to their accuracy. The destructive capabilities and their vulnerability rises as the accuracy of the U.S. nuclear weapons increases. And, indeed, U.S. forces have been given a higher degree of accuracy. The warheads of 300 Minuteman III missiles have been replaced with more accurate, more powerful devices; the addition of the ALCM to the nuclear arsenal has enhanced its overall accuracy, especially after the cruise missile has been furnished with new guidance technique and electronic countermeasures against new Soviet air defenses; and the Trident II (SLBM) has been made more accurate through the addition of a terminal housing system.[5] Nevertheless, as figure 1.2 shows, the United States faces a formidable task and has a long way to go to overcome ICBM vulnerability.

Second, a positive factor for deterrence is the little-known fact that, contrary to widespread opinion, Soviet industrial facilities are more concentrated than those of the United States.[6] Hence, relatively few weapons would be needed for their destruction. Moreover, the Soviet transportation network lacks the duplication of links of the U.S. network and, therefore, is very vulnerable to complete, long-term interruption.

Third, in spite of the improvement in the accuracy of U.S. nuclear weapons, deterrence is weakened by the strong Soviet capability as a result of their high EMT to destroy U.S. silo-based missiles. In other words, the concrete of U.S. silos is not sufficiently hardened to protect the missiles they house. As Soviet missile accuracy is also likely to improve, Moscow will retain a significant advantage over the United States in the 1980s,[7] and this could entail a strong temptation for a first strike, especially while the United States has declared its intention to catch up in the EMT category through the installation of MX missiles.

Fourth, another factor weakening deterrence would be the establishment of an effective anti-ballistic missile (ABM) system. If combined with a massive civil defense organization, it would strengthen the defense to such a degree that deaths and damage caused by nuclear aggression would be reduced to an extent that would tend to destabilize the deterrence principle.[8] If space-based ABM systems could be developed, the same outcome can be anticipated, and the

Figure 1.2 Land-Based ICBM Vulnerability. In order to assure a high probability of destroying a hardened ICBM silo, two high-yield and high-accuracy warheads must be employed. Only the US Minuteman III and the Soviet SS-18 and SS-19 ICBMs carry warheads with the requisite yield and accuracy. As the graph depicts, the US currently has about 1650 warheads deployed on Minuteman IIIs whereas the USSR has over 4800 warheads deployed on SS-18s and SS-19s (assuming maximum tested capability).

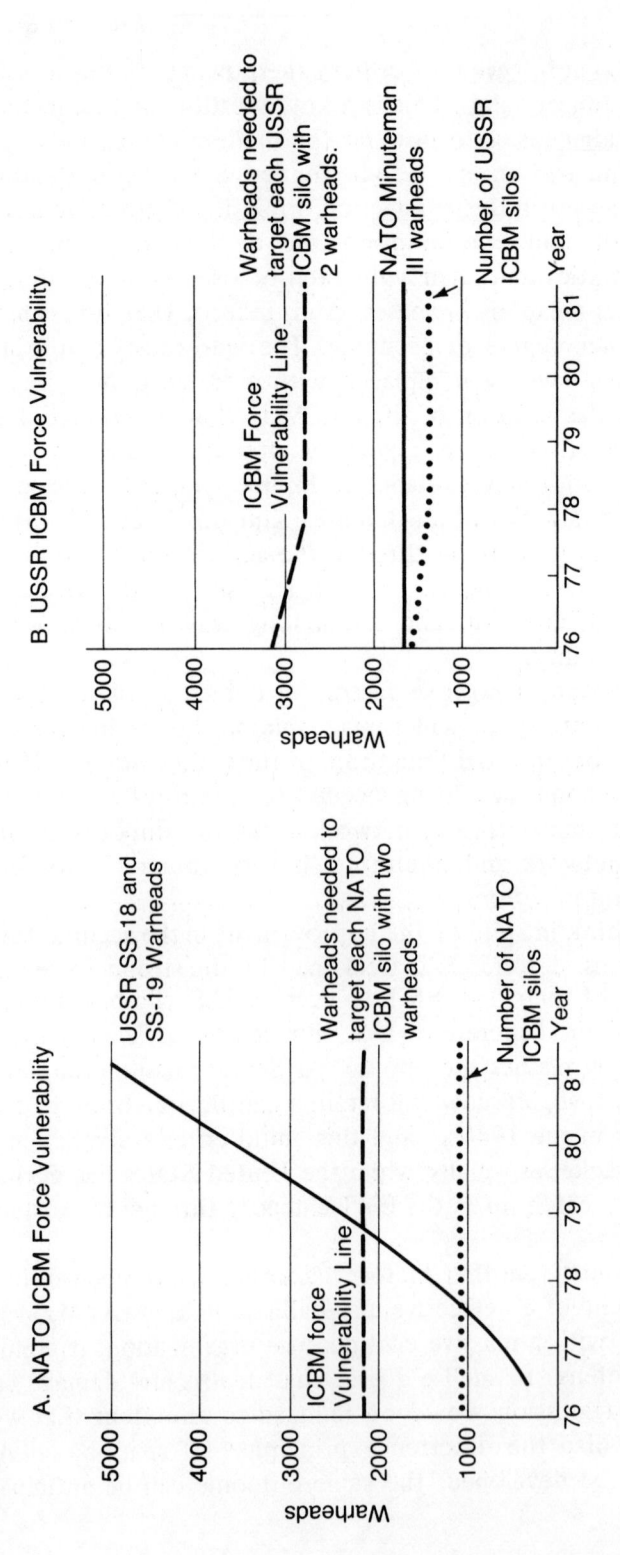

A. NATO ICBM Force Vulnerability

B. USSR ICBM Force Vulnerability

Source: NATO and The Warsaw Pact—Force Comparisons, p. 41.

chances for first strikes by either side may be increased during the development period.

Fifth, effective deterrence depends on the demonstrated ability of the military command and control system, as well as of the national communications network, to withstand the impact of the nuclear exchange. These systems should be sufficiently robust to avoid any temptation by a potential adversary to launch a relatively small strike primarily for the purpose of preventing retaliation later on and then to follow up this first strike with an all-out nuclear attack. In spite of a variety of ground-based, air-based, and satellite-based relay systems to ensure full communications capability, and in spite of at least one Strategic Air Command (SAC) aircraft always being airborne to serve as National Emergency Airborne Command Post (NEACP),[9] communications safety constitutes a continuing vulnerability and requires continued attention to improving the capabilities of the relay systems.

Sixth, effective deterrence depends on the adversary's perceptions of the U.S. credibility of the U.S. threat to engage in nuclear retaliation. This means that the adversary believes in the adequacy of the U.S. nuclear strategic arsenal to inflict pervasive damage, in the resolve of the president to set the nuclear retaliation machinery in motion, and in the capability of the U.S. command and communications system to sustain fully the retaliation sequences that would destroy the adversary's military and industrial facilities and cause millions of casualties. These *perceptions* are critical elements in any serious confrontation, and they include an assessment of how far the American people are prepared to accept enormous devastation and complete change in their accustomed life as a consequence of U.S. retaliatory action.

Soviet Objectives and Fears

Evidence from Russian history going back to the sixteenth century and George Kennan's well-known analysis of the sources of Soviet conduct in the international arena published in 1947[10] suggest significant basic motivations for Soviet foreign policy objectives. Territorial expansion, especially to attain warmwater port access to the oceans of the world, has been a driving force for centuries and remains a Soviet objective today although its pursuit by leaders since the 1917 Revolution has been very cautious as far as the employment of the military is concerned. Equally important as an objective has been the retention of control over territories that have fallen under Soviet domination and influence, particularly in Eastern Europe, and the preservation of worldwide political achievements wherever they have occurred.

The implementation of these Soviet objectives necessitates the pursuit of another crucial goal, namely, to assure maximum security for the Soviet fatherland and for the *cordon sanitaire* that Moscow has created in Eastern Europe and more recently in Afghanistan. Soviet security may also be perceived as threatened by China, with which the USSR has a very long border. All three of Moscow's objectives are essentially strategic and aim at strengthening the political and economic power of the USSR. They provide the needed backdrop for the promotion of ideological aspirations around the globe, with the enhancement of Marxism-Leninism being not only a goal in itself outside the home base, but also a necessary ingredient to hold together and keep going the communist apparatus in the Soviet Union and elsewhere, such as Eastern Europe, Cuba, and Vietnam.

Finally, it is important to note that Soviet domestic and bureaucratic politics furnish strong motivations to support the Soviet objectives outlined above. The Soviet leadership and top-level bureaucracy want to maintain their positions of power, prestige, and profit and their enjoyment of "the good life." Nothing could service this purpose better than an aggressive foreign and security policy that has patriotic overtones and evokes support from lesser bureaucratic elites whose continuing privileges are likely to depend on the continued power of the current leaders in the Politburo and the Central Committee of the Soviet Communist Party.[11]

All these motivations played significant roles in the extraordinary nuclear arms buildup of the Soviet Union. Another contributing factor was and is the need of any top Soviet leader, the General Secretary of the Communist Party, to have the support of the high command of the armed forces to ensure the continuation of his political life and future. Indeed, it is precisely this configuration of politics that makes it possible for the Soviet military establishment to obtain whatever weapons it deems necessary and, therefore, provides one of the dynamics of the escalating nuclear arms race. Of course, in turn, this provides the rationale for equivalent demands by the Pentagon.

There is little doubt that the Soviet nuclear buildup should have dispelled in the minds of the Kremlin leaders any notion of strategic inferiority. Rather, it has created a Soviet advantage and has thereby raised the anxiety level of many Americans, including the Reagan administration. But whether the advantage on the part of the Soviets has given their civilian and military leaders a greater sense of security or whether there is a deeply ingrained obsession with more and more security among these leaders that impels them to increase the numbers and capabilities of their nuclear weapons is difficult to judge. It is fair to assume that unrest and ferment in Poland and other East European satellites strengthen perceptions of insecurity and induce increasing the nuclear arsenal.

Soviet obsession with security should not really be surprising when one considers the invasion of Russia by foreign armies in 1812, 1918, and 1941. Indeed, during the German invasion in World War II, the Soviet armies and regime were almost completely obliterated. Twenty million Soviet citizens died in that war, and, although Moscow is most anxious to protect itself from a similar future catastrophe, these tremendous casualties and vast devastation of their country may have given Soviet leaders a higher level of equanimity when contemplating the horrors of nuclear war than Americans have.

This brings up the important question of how the Soviet leadership views the principle of deterrence for the maintenance of peace. According to Harold Brown: "Soviet military thinking appears to be that the way to deter the United States is to establish superior strategic capability, not merely to be able to destroy some large percentage of U.S. population and industry. Soviet doctrine calls for the ability to wipe out enemy military forces and command-and-control structures as well as urban and industrial targets, and to do all of these more or less simultaneously."[12] This does not suggest Soviet blindness to the catastrophic destruction that would follow a nuclear war. Moscow's intense efforts to have an effective civil defense organization is evidence of that. Nevertheless, some Soviet leaders may view nuclear missiles as decisive weapons in a modern war, and they may consider they will have "won" a strategic nuclear war if the Soviet Union may come out of it with 100 million survivors compared with 50 million in the United States.[13]

Whatever the true sentiments in the Kremlin, Moscow boasts again and again about its singular desire for peace and cooperation with the West. However, full Soviet implementation of the 1975 Final Act of the Conference on Security and Cooperation in Europe (CSCE) leaves much to be desired, and the two follow-up conferences, in Belgrade in 1978 and in Madrid in 1981-83, have mainly produced lots of rhetoric and peace propaganda but little action. The only tangible result of Madrid was the promise of convening a series of meetings. The first of these, in Stockholm in 1984, concentrates on "confidence building and security measures and disarmament of conventional weapons in Europe"; agreement on confidence building measures (CBMs) could be useful for reducing the Soviet obsession with its security, but if past experience is a guide, the prospects for a successful meeting are small. We will return to the subject of CBMs later.

West European Interests, Aspirations, and Fears

A major aspect of U.S. defense policy is the protection of Western Europe from possible Soviet aggression, and, since this involves the maintenance of a vigorous and dependable NATO (North Atlantic Treaty Organization) alliance, U.S. policy makers must be very sensitive to the concerns and interests of our West European allies.

Over the last three decades, the U.S.-West European defense partnership has had its ups and downs, but it is generally recognized that NATO has made an essential contribution to maintaining the peace between the superpowers and in Europe. The NATO treaty obligates the United States to protect Western Europe from a Soviet attack, which, in view of the very large conventional forces possessed by the USSR, seemed to be a continuing possibility and persists at present. The main tool for this protection is the nuclear arsenal of the United States, which serves as a deterring factor against the use of the Soviet Union's conventional military superiority in Europe. Dissuading Soviet leaders from taking advantage of these military opportunities is called extended deterrence, and this kind of deterrence is applicable also to possible Soviet conventional and nuclear aggressive acts against U.S. allies and interests in other parts of the world, especially Japan and South Korea.[14]

During the 1970s, Soviet conventional superiority in Europe was matched by a rapid buildup of nuclear strength through the installation of the SS-20 missiles, each with three nuclear warheads. These missiles, which are categorized as long-range theater nuclear weapons, can be transported with ease and can be relocated on short notice. They have a range of 4,000-5,000 km, and their total number as of the end of 1982 was 345, with 1,035 warheads. These missiles are deployed in the USSR mostly west of the Urals, but some launchers are also located east of these mountains. From the Western USSR they can cover all of Western Europe, but part of Western Europe can also be reached by SS-20 launchers deployed east of the Urals.

While the older Soviet long-range nuclear theater weapons (SS-4 and SS-5) are being gradually phased out, a newer bomber (the Backfire) is being deployed in larger numbers. It is a modern, basically intermediate-range aircraft that can carry four nuclear weapons, has supersonic speed, and is based mostly in the Western USSR. With refueling, it could undertake intercontinental missions. Other aircraft deployed against Western Europe are the Badger (subsonic) and Blinder (supersonic).

Although the United States has thousands of short-range tactical nuclear weapons in Europe, in terms of long-range theater nuclear weapons, NATO is substantially inferior to the Soviet and Warsaw Pact forces. Table 1.2 clearly demonstrates this. The British and French forces included in this table are not considered to be theater weapons in the strict sense; at the same time, they are aging and are undergoing modernization. The Vulcan bomber is nearing obsolescence, and the U.S. F-111s are also quite old. Nevertheless, table 1.2 shows a 4.6 to 1 Warsaw Pact superiority to NATO in warheads and a 3.2 to 1 superiority in launchers. And perhaps surprisingly, even in the shorter-range nuclear weapons category (ranges 100-1,000 miles), the Warsaw Pact enjoys a 2.7 to 1 superiority to NATO in warheads and bombs and a 2.6 to 1 advantage in launchers.[15] Only in tube artillery firing nuclear shells (very short-range nuclear weapons) does NATO have a substantial advantage over the Warsaw Pact.[16]

The trend toward the development of Soviet superiority in theater nuclear weapons vis à vis NATO was recognized and deplored by the governments of the European NATO allies. At the suggestion of former West German Chancellor Helmut Schmidt and with the full endorsement of the U.S. government, the NATO Council decided in December 1979 to reestablish some kind of balance in the long-range theater nuclear weapons field by beginning to deploy at the end of 1983 108 U.S. Pershing II and 464 ground-launched cruise missiles (GLCMs). At the same time, negotiations were to be initiated between Washington and Moscow aiming at an arms control agreement not only halting the continued deployment of SS-20s but dismantling at least some of those missiles already installed. If that effort were to be successful, the number of new NATO weapons could be reduced, or there would perhaps be no need for any deployment.

At the time of this writing, the negotiating efforts have not been successful, and the first Pershing II and cruise missiles were installed in December 1983. Shortly thereafter, the Soviets walked out of the Geneva negotiations. In this connection, it should be noted that there is now a successor to the SS-20, the SS-21, which is being stationed in the German Democratic Republic. Other new successor models under construction by the Soviet Union are the SS-22 and SS-23. It

Table 1.2. Comparison of WTO and NATO Theater Nuclear Weapons in Europe

	Type	Launchers	Warheads/Bombs
WTO	SS-20	345	1,035
	SS-5	16	16
	SS-4	275	275
Total Missiles		636	1,326
	Backfire	100	400
	Badger	310	620
	Blinder	125	250
Total Bombers		535	1,270
Total		1,171	2,596
NATO	Polaris (UK)	64	64
	M-20 (FR)	80	80
	SSBS S-2 (FR)	18	18
	Pershing II (US)	25	25*
Total Missiles		187	187
	Vulcan B-2 (US)	48	96
	F-111 E/F (US)	156	312
Total Bombers		204	408
Total		391	595

*Twenty-five Pershing II Long Range Theatre Nuclear Forces missiles were deployed as of December 31, 1983. Plans call for deployment of a total of 108 Pershing IIs and 464 GLCMs by 1988.

Sources: Adapted from Carnesale, et al., *Living With Nuclear Weapons* (New York: Bantam Books, 1983), p. 120 and Department of Defense, Soviet Military Power, 1984, pp. 21, 51.

is important to note that the initiative for the development of all three new missiles was taken before the 1979 NATO so-called double-trade decision.[17]

NATO's intention to deploy the Pershing IIs and cruise missiles has evoked considerable opposition among substantial segments of the populations of Great Britain, the Netherlands, and West Germany. It has been a major cause of the creation of new or the revitalization of existing peace movements in these countries and elsewhere in Western Europe. Although the origins of these have varied—religious groups, ecologists, left wings of socialist parties, communist fellow travelers—the proposed installation of the new U.S. weapons served as a focal point of cooperation for the movement leaders. It is very doubtful that the adherents and supporters of the peace movements represent the majority of the people in their respective countries. Nevertheless, they have had an impact on thinking and politics, and this needs to be taken into account by congressional decision makers on defense issues. The peace movements and the fear of nuclear war have also spawned new intellectual approaches on both sides of the Atlantic to prevent such a catastrophe in Europe by strengthening the conventional capabilities of NATO forces to counter successfully any aggressive Soviet moves. These approaches included the question whether the West should renounce a first nuclear strike, as proposed by George Kennan and Robert McNamara.[18] Although such renunciation has been rejected by U.S., British, and West German scholars, this increase in NATO conventional capabilities remains an attractive option in spite of its high cost and the possible need to reintroduce conscription in the United States and Great Britain.[19]

Meanwhile, the large demonstrations staged by the peace movements in West Germany, the Netherlands, and Great Britain have created apprehension, especially in the Federal Republic, about violence and turmoil that may be caused when the actual deployment of the U.S. weapons takes place. The conservative government of Helmut Kohl in Bonn has strengthened the antidemonstration laws in West Germany while hoping and working for a last-minute agreement between the United States and the Soviet Union in the negotiations on the theater nuclear weapons. The tensions created by this issue are compounded by trade problems between Washington and the European Economic Community on a variety of protectionist and competition issues in international commerce, including subsidized sales of agricultural commodities around the world, dumping of European steel products in the United States, and business with the Soviet Union.

Although the majority of Europeans realizes that peace and their freedom depend on the extended nuclear deterrence provided by the United States, many perceive their roles as junior partners in NATO with some degree of displeasure. While the consultation process among the NATO allies seems to have improved, Europeans resent that procurement of military equipment and weapons continues to favor U.S. producers. Many are also resentful that the United States has abolished conscription whereas on the Continent the member states continue obligatory military service for their young men. A number of West Germans complain and have filed suit before the Constitutional Court that once the Pershings II and GLCMs are in place, the power of making war will shift from Bonn to Washington, implying a derogation of West German sovereignty. French Foreign Minister Claude Cheysson characterized the relationship between the United States and Western Europe in 1982 as that of two parties that "no longer speak the same language. They are increasingly incapable of understanding each other's policy and mistrust between them is on the increase."[20] Although this statement is clearly an exaggeration and does not reflect the 1983/84 mood, billion-dollar decisions in Washington on supermissiles, neutron devices, radiation weapons, and nerve gas rack the nerves of many Europeans who see themselves as the most likely victims of the expanding arsenal. They reject the U.S. claim that, for example, nerve gas, a barbarous and internationally proscribed weapon, must be manufactured solely to force the Soviet Union, which also has this weapon, to disarm. In this connection, a respected German newspaper makes the following comments, which congressional defense policy makers may want to ponder:

> We risk being wiped out as a species if this deterrent fails to work, by either a miscalculation or a technical mishap.
>
> The superpowers have an enormous responsibility for the survival of mankind, and so far they have not done it justice.
>
> This is the intellectual and political background against which the peace movement all over the world is gaining stature and support.
>
> It will certainly succeed in doing so if it manages to steer clear of political violence and communist manipulation.
>
> Détente as a military means of keeping world peace is breaking down under the impact of progress in arms technology.
>
> What is needed is a change in political thinking that does justice to the growing danger mankind faces.[21]

If such sentiments are widespread, commitment to the common defense could well be weakened. And, indeed, public opinion polls taken in 1983 suggest fairly strong inclinations toward neutralism in several important NATO countries. Table 1.3 provides the pertinent figures, with West Germany showing the greatest propensity toward neutrality. Nevertheless, deployment of the Pershing II and cruise missiles was supported by narrow margins in West Germany (37 to 35 percent), France (34 to 29 percent), and Great Britain (43 to 34 percent). It was opposed in the Netherlands.[22] Moreover, in spite of the neutralist tendencies, favorable opinions of the United States outnumbered unfavorable ones by a margin of two to one, at least in 1981,[23] and more respondents in the four countries considered it better to belong to NATO than to get out. For details consult table 1.4.

Table 1.3. Growing Neutralism (1983)

Question:	Some have said that Western Europe would be safer if it moved toward neutralism in the East-West conflict. Others argue that such a move would be dangerous. Would you, yourself, favor or oppose a move toward neutralism in Western Europe?

	Favor	Oppose
West Germany	57%	43%
Netherlands	53	32
Great Britain	45	42
France	43	41

Source: Adapted from surveys by the Gallup Organization for *Newsweek*, January 31, 1983. (Number interviewed: between 500 and 754 in each country.)

As for the current international tensions, 38 percent blamed the Soviet military buildup, but a substantial portion of the Europeans cited the increase in U.S. military strength (24 percent) and aggressive U.S. policies toward the Soviet Union (23 percent).[24]

Finally, how much confidence do West Europeans have that the United States will approach global problems in a reasonable manner? A substantial majority of West Germans and a small majority of Italians have great or fair confidence. But a strong majority of the French feel otherwise. However, if the security of their countries were actually

Table 1.4. The Attractiveness of NATO (1981)

Question:	All things considered, do you think it is better for [the country] to belong to NATO, that is, the North Atlantic Treaty Organization, or would it be better for us to get out of NATO and become a neutral country.

	Better to belong		Better to get out	
	March 1981	July 1981	March 1981	July 1981
West Germany	67%	64%	14%	18%
Great Britain	67	59	20	29
Netherlands	62	56	17	25
Italy	60	49	30	42
France*	45	33	40	51

*In France the question referred to the Atlantic Alliance instead of NATO.
Source: USIA Survey.

Table 1.5. Confidence in U.S. Global Policy and Reliability as a Military Ally (1982)

Question: How much confidence do you have generally in the United States to deal with global problems in a reasonable manner?

	Great Britain	France	West Germany	Italy	Belgium
Very much	6%	4%	16%	17%	7%
Fairly much	29	36	41	36	38
Not very much	39	35	33	18	20
None whatsoever	21	12	7	11	10
No opinion	5	13	3	18	25

Question: If the security of your country were threatened by a Soviet attack, how much confidence would you have in such an event that the United States would do everything necessary for the defense of your country, even at the risk that the United States would be subjected to a direct attack?

	Great Britain	West Germany	Belgium	Denmark
Very much	20%	17%	12%	17%
Fairly much	36	45	34	32
Not very much	28	27	23	25
None whatsoever	12	8	10	11
No opinion	4	3	21	15

Question: How much confidence do you have in the capability of NATO to defend Western Europe against attack?

	Great Britain	France	West Germany	Italy	Belgium
Very much	12%	5%	16%	16%	7%
Fairly much	44	34	45	33	36
Not very much	25	29	29	19	24
None whatsoever	10	9	6	9	9
No opinion	9	23	4	23	24

Source: Adapted from Gallup International Survey published by *Newsweek*, March 15, 1982. (Number interviewed: over 6,000 in the countries listed plus Switzerland)

threatened by a Soviet attack, there is considerable confidence that the United States would do everything necessary for the defense of these countries even at the risk of a direct attack on U.S. territory. Moreover, the West Germans, British, and Belgians have strong confidence in NATO's capability to defend Western Europe against aggression, and this is also the view of substantial minorities in Italy and France. For details see table 1.5.

All this suggests the complexity of the U.S.-West European relationship. It also points up the problems in developing appropriate U.S. defense policies amidst the many crosscurrents of interests, fears, and aspirations among the NATO allies and the enormous task congressional decision makers may have in coming up with a balanced judgment.

EAST-WEST SOLUTIONS

Congressional budgetary inputs and advice with respect to U.S. defense policy must take into consideration the status of East-West relations and the possibility of bringing about a change in this relationship if this should promote the national interest. During the first two years of the Reagan administration, U.S.-Soviet relations, the centerpiece of the East-West relationship, were highly confrontational. Reagan's pervasive anticommunism produced a number of highly publicized statements that were received in the Kremlin with utmost displeasure. He characterized the Soviet Union as engaging in immoral, underhanded practices and duplicity in international politics and asserted repeatedly—though perhaps with justification—that the USSR is in deep economic difficulty and that "the march of freedom and democracy . . . will leave Marxism-Leninism on the ash heap of history."[25]

Since World War II, the nature of the East-West relationship has varied. Periods of extreme confrontation alternated with periods of cooperation and détente. The second half of the 1940s and much of the 1950s were marked by several instances of harsh confrontation, the period of the Cold War, although several attempts were made by both sides to seek some kind of accommodation. In 1952, the Soviet Union proposed talks with the United States, Great Britain, and France on a German peace treaty, including possible German reunification and rearmament, although a rearmed Germany would have to be neutralized. In addition, the Soviet government held out the prospect for a fifty-year European security treaty. Perhaps significantly, this proposal, articulated before Stalin's death in 1953, was made during a period of overwhelming U.S. strategic superiority over the Soviet Union. When a foreign ministers' conference of the four powers was finally held in early 1954, the Soviet Union backed away from a unified but neutralized Germany.[26] In 1953, it had mastered the technology of the hydrogen bomb and was pressing forward with its nuclear buildup. A summit conference of the four powers held in Geneva in 1955, which was attended by President

Eisenhower and Soviet Premier Bulganin, and which earlier had been very much desired by the Soviet leadership, turned out to be a relaxed get-together, which, however, made little progress in solving any major problems between East and West.

The Geneva summit of 1955 was followed in 1959 by the visit of Nikita Khrushchev, first secretary of the Soviet Communist Party and Soviet premier (chairman of the Council of Ministers) to Camp David for consultations with Eisenhower. Khrushchev's trip to the United States was remarkable in that it included lunches with film stars, a visit to Eisenhower's farm at Gettysburg, and a farewell address to the American people on television. Hopes were high that the confrontational period between the two superpowers was coming to an end. But, while Khrushchev was clearly committed to "peaceful coexistence," it did not mean the abandonment of basic Soviet foreign policy goals or an end to the ideological and economic struggle between the Soviet Union and the Western democracies. The primary concern was the repudiation of war as a means of solving controversial issues.[27]

What had been dubbed the spirit of Camp David did not last long. Eisenhower and Khrushchev had agreed to meet again in May 1960 in Paris, for another summit of the big four powers, and later in Moscow. Problems with Western access to Berlin and the Soviet threat of signing a peace treaty with its East German satellite darkened the prospect for continuing on the path of détente. However, it was the downing of a U.S. U-2 spy plane within the Soviet Union that scuttled the meeting of Eisenhower and Khrushchev in Paris, although both leaders had actually traveled to that city. Khrushchev demanded an apology from Eisenhower for the overflight, which the latter was unwilling to extend.[28] Although it is far from sure whether any benefits for peace and for a better relationship between the superpowers could have been derived from the Paris meeting, as things turned out, it was not surprising that the confrontational climate reemerged. Containment of the Soviet Union remained the primary preoccupation of U.S. policy makers.

While cooperative U.S. and Soviet behavior was manifested in the Antarctica and Limited Nuclear Test Ban treaties as well as in the establishment of the hot line, in-depth consideration of détente policy did not surface until 1967.

U.S. Acquiescence to Detente

Pressures for improved relations between the West and the Soviet Union emanating from European elites such as the Action Committee for the United States of Europe found only a cautious response from President Kennedy, who declared in July 1963, "In time the unity of the West can lead to the unity of East and West."[29] In 1966, President Johnson followed this line of thought guardedly when he stated that NATO, the Atlantic Alliance, must adapt to changing conditions, including quickening the progress in East-West relations.[30]

NATO became indeed the forum within which the basis for a joint U.S.-West European détente policy was placed. At the December 1967 meeting of the NATO Council, the so-called Harmel Report was approved (Pierre Harmel was the Belgian foreign minister). This report declared:

> Military security and a policy of détente are not contradictory but complementary.... Each Ally should play its full part in promoting an improvement in relations with the Soviet Union and the other countries of Eastern Europe, bearing in mind that the pursuit of détente must not be allowed to split the Alliance.... The relaxation of tensions is not the final goal but is part of a long-term process to promote better relations.... The ultimate political purpose of the Alliance is to achieve a just and lasting peaceful order in Europe accompanied by appropriate security guarantees.[31]

The Soviet invasion of Czechoslovakia in 1968 to suppress by armed force an indigenous movement toward political liberalization quickly dispelled in Western Europe much of the euphoria surrounding the Harmel-inspired détente initiative. However, this reaction did not last long, and within a few months the pursuit of détente resumed in Western Europe, although the United States remained much more lukewarm toward this effort.

The Harmel Report spawned another initiative with potentially significant implications for détente. An attempt was undertaken to reduce the conventional forces of NATO and the Warsaw Pact countries in a mutual and balanced manner. Negotiations on mutual and balanced force reductions (MBFR) began in Vienna in 1973 and are still in progress. All members of NATO except France, Portugal, and Iceland are participants.

In response to repeated Soviet requests, NATO set up machinery in 1970 to coordinate the views of the NATO allies for meetings to prepare for substantive discussions on European security and cooperation to be held in Helsinki in 1972 and in Geneva in 1973. Although the United States initially wanted to link these negotiations with positive results in the MBFR talks, it later abandoned this attempt at linkage. The results of the Conference on Security and Cooperation in Europe, as stipulated in the Final Act signed August 1, 1975 in Helsinki, contained confidence-building measures based on exchanges of information about military activities such as impending maneuvers, agreements dealing with economic cooperation, and a chapter concerning humanitarian issues and freedom of information.

To monitor the implementation of CSCE, a follow-up meeting took place in Belgrade between October 1977 and March 1978. Although there was much controversy during that meeting about what, if any, progress was achieved, a decision was taken to continue the CSCE process and to hold another follow-up meeting in Madrid, which began in November 1980 and, after a long adjournment in 1981, ended in 1983. Events in Poland after the declaration of martial law in December 1981 have focused attention on violations of the Helsinki Agreement in Eastern Europe and have cast a pall of gloom and disappointment over this phase of détente, especially in the United States.

Doubts about the Value of Detente

Many Americans have been suspicious of détente as being a tactic through which the Soviet Union is gaining considerably more advantages than the West, advantages that could not be achieved through other, especially Soviet, economic and technological resources. In very conservative quarters, a tough, confrontational stance toward the Soviet Union is seen as the only means to deal with Moscow and obtain concessions. Indeed, when during the Republican presidential primaries in 1976 Ronald Reagan challenged President Ford's foreign policies toward the Soviet Union as not being tough enough, the latter ordered his campaign organization to drop the word *detente* from the description of his foreign policies.

For President Nixon and Secretary of State Kissinger, however, détente was an important part of U.S. foreign policy. They considered détente based on strict reciprocity to be in the national interest.[32] For Kissinger, "detente could never replace a balance of power; it would be the result of equilibrium, not a substitute for it."[33] Yet, he acknowledged that the quest for détente or peaceful coexistence had its perils, but it did not follow from this that a "crusading policy of confrontation would prove more successful. The former might sap our vigilance; the latter would risk our national cohesion and our alliance as our government would be denounced with increasing vehemence as the cause of international tensions."[34]

According to Kissinger, the U.S. strategy of détente required the provisions of incentives and penalties in order to restrain the Soviets from the temptation of expansionism.[35] In other words, U.S. resistance to expansionism was to be linked to reciprocal cooperation with Moscow.

During the period of deepening détente beginning in 1967, increasing cooperation between the United States and the Soviet Union was reflected in the conclusion of a number of agreements designed to limit the possibility of nuclear war. These accords were the Outer Space Treaty of 1967, the Nuclear Non-Proliferation Treaty of 1968, the Seabed Arms Control Treaty of 1971, the Strategic Arms Limitation Treaty (SALT) of 1972, the Treaty on the Limitation of Underground Nuclear Weapons Tests of 1974, the Vladivostok Agreement of 1974 placing a ceiling on delivery vehicles, and the Peaceful Nuclear Explosion Treaty of 1976. However, President Carter's attempt to obtain Moscow's agreement to further lowering the limits on strategic nuclear weapons failed in the SALT II negotiations, and the prospects for even a less ambitious agreement faded away in the wake of the invasion of Afghanistan by the Soviets. At the same time, the level of superpower confrontation rose rapidly, and this trend accelerated further under President Reagan. Nevertheless, the United States agreed to participate in a 35-nation Conference on Security and Disarmament in Stockholm in January 1984. With the Soviets having broken off all negotiations on the control of strategic and theater nuclear weapons as well as on the MBFR talks, as a protest against U.S. deployment of Pershing IIs and ALCMs in December 1983, there was some U.S. hope that the Stockholm talks might be a means to bring Moscow back to the negotiating table. However, these hopes were not fulfilled.

THE NUCLEAR DILEMMA AND EAST-WEST ACCOMMODATIONS

When one considers the *numerical* imbalance in strategic and theater nuclear weapons favoring the Soviet Union, two questions arise that must be addressed by congressional defense experts and by Congress as a whole in its budgeting deliberations. First, can a new approach to dealing with the Soviet Union help in bringing about a more accommodating attitude in the Soviet leadership with respect to nuclear arms control? Clearly, Moscow holds one of the keys to reducing the prospect of a nuclear clash between the superpowers, and the history of U.S.-Soviet relations shows that there are common interests of the two countries and that beneficial policies can be pursued if these interests are carefully identified and recognized. Second, what is the *realistic* parity that U.S. policy must attempt to achieve? Setting excessive objectives can be counterproductive to achieving U.S. and West European security, especially in view of Moscow's paranoiac fears and obsession with its own security.

The Reagan administration has issued calls for "constructive East-West relations" and they were repeated again after Breshnev's death, but they were said to depend on "constructive Soviet behavior."[36] What is meant by "constructive behavior" can be best understood by what the State Department regards as objectionable. In an overview of U.S.-Soviet relations, the Bureau of Public Affairs lists the following Soviet activities as falling into this category:

> A continuing quest for military superiority;
> An unconstructive involvement in unstable regions of the world;
> The unrelenting effort to impose an alien Soviet "model" on nominally independent Soviet clients and allies, particularly Poland;
> The continuing practice of stretching a series of treaties and agreements to the brink of violation and, in some cases, beyond; and
> A consistently poor record on human rights, which contravenes Soviet obligations under the Helsinki accords.[37]

Nevertheless, the State Department document regards direct negotiations and dialogue with Moscow on major issues as necessary for peace. The U.S. agenda suggested for such negotiations includes:

> Seeking improvement in Soviet human rights performance;
> Reducing armaments through verifiable agreements and easing the burdens of military spending;
> Managing and resolving regional conflicts; and
> Improving economic and other bilateral relations based on reciprocity and mutual interest.[38]

The opening of new consulates in both countries and the revival of cultural exchanges with the Soviet Union have also provided recent topics of discussion. However, whether the conditions set for U.S.-Soviet negotiations by Washington are acceptable to Moscow is doubtful. In his first speech after becoming Brezhnev's successor, Yuri Andropov stated: "We know full well that the imperialists will never meet one's pleas for peace. It can be upheld only resting upon the invincible might of the Soviet armed forces."[39] Nevertheless, despite this disparity, the general climate for negotiations improved somewhat in 1983. A five-year grain purchase agreement was signed that provides substantial benefits to U.S. farmers and Soviet consumers, and the Reagan administration lifted the embargo on the sale of pipe-laying equipment for the continued construction of the Soviet-West European natural gas pipeline. Embargoes on the sale of both grain and pipe-laying equipment had hurt the United States more than the Soviet Union. With the death of Andropov in late 1983, it is uncertain at this writing what future relations will be like under his successor, Konstantin Chernenko.

The question of when substantial parity between the U.S. and Soviet arsenals of strategic and theater nuclear weapons exists is complicated and controversial. As far as the strategic weapons are concerned, the Union of Concerned Scientists believes parity prevails because of the slightly larger number of U.S. warheads and the improved accuracy of the new Trident missile. On the other hand, figures discussed earlier in this chapter on launchers and destructive power give credence to the claim of the administration that the Soviet Union has superiority and seeks to maintain it. A Gallup survey released in January 1983 suggests that Americans believe the nuclear arms gap to be closing and that they are less favorably disposed toward increasing defense spending than at any other time during the last ten years.[40]

With respect to theater weapons, the evidence of Soviet superiority is more clear-cut. With the approach of the deadline for the deployment of the Pershing II and cruise missiles, the negotiating pace on an acceptable weapons balance and arms control mechanism became more intensive. On August 28, 1983, Yuri Andropov offered to destroy the number of medium-range missiles, including the SS-20, by which Soviet nuclear missiles exceed those of Britain and France, which in 1983 numbered 162, in return for a commitment by the United States not to install its weapons.[41] But, while the Soviet Union insisted that the British and French missiles must be taken into account in any U.S.-Soviet agreement, Washington has insisted with equal vigor that these are not under NATO control and therefore cannot be counted. We will return to this argument later in this volume; suffice it here to mention that for many Europeans and some Americans the position of the United States on this issue is weak.

Whatever the outcome of the internal debate about parity of nuclear weapons, it is imperative for peace that the United States and its NATO allies talk to the Soviets at every level with patience and understanding. We must take into account the history of the Russian people, the obsession of the Czars and now of their Communist heirs with internal and external security. It makes little sense to insult the Soviet leaders and indirectly the Russian people because it cannot be our aim to drive the Russians further into nationalistic and military introversion. As for concern about the military balance, the former British foreign secretary Lord Carrington said that we must know when enough is enough.[42] At the same time, Moscow must be convinced that new, beneficial opportunities for cooperation could arise if it were to put a stop to expansionism.

Many of the views expressed in the preceding paragraph came from a lecture by Lord Carrington, former foreign secretary in the Thatcher government, to the International Institute for Strategic Studies. We would like to close this section with some very appropriate comments by Lord Carrington on how talks with the Soviet leaders should be conducted.

> These talks should be conducted in an atmosphere of calm confidence, and ... the broader political dimension of East/West relations should be constantly at the forefront of the Western mind. It would be wrong to approach these important negotiations on the military defensive—on the military alert—and for our dialogue with the East to be hagridden by fear of military inferiority.
>
> It is my view that one of the reasons for the upsurge of nuclear debate in the West is that this mood of sobriety and calm resolution has not always been encouraged by Western governments.
>
> The West will make a major mistake if it reduces East/West diplomacy to nothing but nuclear accountancy. Public opinion is understandably concerned when the raw nerve of nuclear competition is overexposed. We must be seen to be taking the broad view. The dehumanisation of the East/West relationship would be the quickest road to catastrophe I can imagine.[43]

THE U.S. MILITARY: INTERESTS AND MANAGEMENT PERFORMANCE

The deliberations of Congress on defense and budgetary matters are subjected to lobbying by the Pentagon and the armed forces in support of maximum increases of the military budgets. These pressures on Congress are motivated not only by the quest for enhanced U.S. security but also by understandable interests in promoting opportunities for the uniformed personnel that open up when the size of the navy, air force, and army is expanded. In addition, the prestige and influence of the leadership of the military establishment are strengthened. President Reagan and Defense Secretary Caspar Weinberger have always vigorously supported the demands of the armed forces for the rapid "rearmament" of the United States. It is interesting to note that former President Gerald Ford, in the summer of 1983, expressed opposition to the unrelenting increases in the defense budget. His reason was concern about the enormous budget deficit running in excess of $200 billion in 1984 and several years to follow.[44] Fears have been expressed by some observers that the continuing high deficits may destroy the economic health of the United States and perhaps the industrialized world and, thereby, may constitute a more serious threat to the United States than Soviet aggression.

While there is general agreement that the deficits are intolerable if they persist, a formidable coalition of various constituencies shares the interests of the armed forces in higher defense expenditures. This coalition consists of the large and small U.S. compaines that are defense contractors and subcontractors and whose operation and profits depend on a continuing stream of orders for military hardware. Stockholders of these firms also have an interest in expanded military budgets; apprehension about a slowdown in defense budget increases has had a negative effect on the stock prices of companies prominently engaged in defense work.

Another segment of the defense support coalition is organized labor, which has an interest in achieving and keeping maximum employment in defense contractor plants that are unionized. Finally, all communities with military facilities are anxious to see military and civilian employment in their facilities as high as possible and, therefore, have a stake in high defense budgets. All this means pervasive pressure in Congress in support of expanding the U.S. military establishment and a more difficult task for congressional defense experts to come up with a rational analysis and evaluation of the Pentagon's budgetary demands and true military needs. For example, are additional aircraft carriers a sound military investment? Can we afford the B-1 bomber when the more effective "stealth" bomber may become operational only a few years later? In this connection, we need to draw attention again to the change of mood of the general public, a net majority of which thinks that defense spending is too high (41 percent, vs. 16 percent who consider it too low).[45]

U.S. military expenditures are affected by the management capabilities of the Pentagon and the armed services and, therefore, the formulation of defense policy and the budget must take into consideration the quality of management performance. During 1983, a number of newspaper reports surfaced about the very high prices paid by the different services to suppliers for items that could have been purchased on the open market at a fraction of the price.[46] Secretary Weinberger has attempted to stamp out this incredible waste and inefficiency, but how far he has succeeded, given the mammoth size of the armed forces operations, is doubtful.

Another management problem is the selection of new weapons systems. What is the probability of the new systems working with full effectiveness, or are they likely to be marginally effective? How much do new weapons systems duplicate existing weapons? How realistic are the cost estimates for new weapons, and what is the probability of extensive cost overruns? The Department of Defense (DOD) has a poor record in controlling escalating weapons costs: in 1983, according to the Congressional Budget Office, of 60 major weapons being built, 35 showed significant real growth in unit costs.[47] Because of the budgetary responsibility Congress has in determining the final shape of the U.S. defense posture, the creation of a Congressional Office of Defense Appraisal (CODA) has been suggested.[48] This organization could provide a centralized, coherent integration of U.S. military strategy, available resources, and military spending. Undoubtedly, the creation of such an office would be opposed by the national security bureaucracy since it would severely constrain the discretion now enjoyed by this bureaucracy, which claims superior knowledge and expertise in defense matters. But, since CODA could possibly save billions of dollars and reduce the vast budget deficits, its establishment might be in the national interest.

This chapter has discussed the many forces at work and some of the intellectual crosscurrents affecting the making of U.S. defense policy. The mixed signals reflected in the foregoing discussion have different kinds of relevance for and impact on the various parts of the decision-making apparatus through which Congress performs its constitutional duty to raise and support the military forces of the United States. This apparatus will be discussed and analyzed in the next chapter.

NOTES

1. Luigi Barzini, *The Europeans* (New York: Simon & Schuster, 1983), p. 219.
2. Henry Kissinger, *White House Years* (Boston: Little, Brown, 1979), p. 552.

3. Albert Carnesale et al. (the Harvard Nuclear Study Group), *Living with Nuclear Weapons* (New York: Bantam Books, 1983), p. 121. For a detailed description of the ALCM capabilities see Center for Defense Information, *Defense Monitor* 12, 4 (1983): 2 and 3.

4. David C. Jones, chairman of the Joint Chiefs of Staff, *United States Military Posture for FY 1982* (Department of Defense, Joint Chiefs of Staff, 1982), p. 25.

5. Ibid., p. 2, and Carnesale, *Living with Nuclear Weapons*, p. 122.

6. Ibid., p. 123.

7. Jones, *United States Military Posture*, p. 26.

8. See Harold Brown, *Thinking about National Security* (Boulder, Colo.: Westview Press, 1983), p. 56.

9. Ibid., pp. 76-77.

10. George F. Kennan [X, pseudonym], "The Sources of Soviet Conduct," *Foreign Affairs* 25 (July 1946): 566-82.

11. For details of this phenomenon see Werner Feld, *Reunification and West German-Soviet Relations* (The Hague: Nijhoff, 1963), p. 81.

12. Brown, *Thinking about National Security*, p. 54.

13. Ibid.

14. Carnesale, *Living with Nuclear Weapons*, pp. 139-40; and Brown, *Thinking about National Security*, p. 56.

15. Carnesale, *Living with Nuclear Weapons*, p. 130.

16. *NATO and the Warsaw Pact—Force Comparisons*, figure 19 (Brussels: NATO, 1982) p. 40.

17. *Handelsblatt*, July 15, 1983.

18. McGeorge Bundy, George F. Kennan, Robert S. McNamara, Gerard Smith, "Nuclear Weapons and the Atlantic Alliance," *Foreign Affairs* 60, 4 (1982): 753-68.

19. See European Security Study, *Strengthening Conventional Deterrence in Europe* (New York: St. Martin's Press, 1983).

20. Quoted in *Die Zeit*, July 30, 1982.

21. *Der Tagesspiegel*, July 17, 1983.

22. William Schneider, "Elite and Public Opinion: The Alliance's New Fissure?" *Public Opinion* (February/March 1983), pp. 5 ff., on p. 5.

23. Ibid., p. 6.

24. Ibid., and *International Herald Tribune*, October 25, 1982, pp. 1-2.

25. U.S. Department of State, Bureau of Public Affairs, *Promoting Democracy and Peace* (Current Policy, No. 399), June 8, 1982.

26. Adam Ulam, *Expansion and Coexistence: Soviet Foreign Policy 1917-1973* (New York: Praeger, 1973), pp. 535-40.

27. For additional details see Richard C. Gripp, *Patterns of Soviet Politics* (Homewood, Ill.: Dorsey Press, 1973), pp. 295-97.

28. Details are found in Dwight D. Eisenhower, *Waging Peace* (Garden City, N.Y.: Doubleday, 1965), pp. 546-58.

29. Quoted in Elliot R. Goodman, *The Fate of the Atlantic Community* (New York: Praeger, 1975), p. 296.

30. Address by President Lyndon B. Johnson at New York, October 7, 1966, *Department of State Bulletin*, Vol. 55, No. 1426, pp. 623-24.

31. *NATO Handbook* (February 1976), p. 64.

32. Kissinger, *The White House Years*, p. 949.

33. Ibid., p. 1143.

34. Ibid., p. 1256.

35. Ibid., p. 1144.

36. William G. Hyland, "U.S.-Soviet Relations, The Long Road Back," *Foreign Affairs* 60, 3 (Winter 1981): 525-50.

37. U.S. Department of State, Bureau of Public Affairs, *GIST*, July 1983.

38. Ibid.

39. *Times-Picayune* (New Orleans), November 13, 1982.

40. *Gallup Report*, January 1983, No. 208, pp. 10-14.

41. *Times-Picayune* (New Orleans), August 29, 1983.

42. This quotation is from a thoughtful article by Lord Carrington, "Lack of Consistent Political Strategy: A Cause of Friction," *NATO Review* 31, 2 (1983): 1-6, on p. 4.

43. Ibid., p. 3.

44. *Times-Picayune* (New Orleans), August 28, 1983.

45. *Gallup Report*, January 1983, No. 208, p. 12.

46. See for example *Time*, July 25, 1983, p. 16.

47. Center for Defense Information, *Defense Monitor* 12, 2 (1983): 4.

48. Ibid., p. 3.

2
CONGRESSIONAL ORGANIZATION AND PROCESS REGARDING DEFENSE ISSUES

The U.S. Constitution has divided the authority to formulate national defense policy between the president and Congress. The president is designated as the commander-in-chief of the armed forces, and (with Senate confirmation) he appoints the highest military leaders. Congress is empowered by the Constitution to "provide for the common defense"; to "declare war"; to "raise and support armies"; to "provide and maintain" the navy; and to promulgate rules and regulations governing the armed forces (Article I, Section 8). Finally, a fundamental principle of the U.S. constitutional framework is the notion of "civilian supremacy" over the armed forces, which implies that it is up to civilian policy makers to determine whether, when, and where U.S. armed forces are to be employed.[1] Moreover, the secretary of defense and the secretaries of the army, navy, and air force, as well as their deputies, are usually civilians, which strengthens the principle of civilian supremacy.

Since the early 1970s, Congress has been increasingly assertive in injecting itself into the formulation of U.S. defense policy, not only as far as the large outlines are concerned but also in the execution of specific military operations. Congress insisted on the termination of the war in Vietnam and advocated the limitation of U.S. military intervention in El Salvador. It sounded growing alarm about the involvement of the U.S. "peace-keeping" forces in the hostilities in Lebanon, which, as a result of deteriorating military circumstances in that country, the administration was eventually forced to withdraw in early 1984.

The most important instrument for injecting Congress's interests and wishes into the formulation of defense policy is the power of the purse. Since the Pentagon budget requests in the mid-1980s are likely to be $300 billion or more, the influence Congress can exert through the appropriations process is awesome. It can determine which weapons and equipment can be purchased. It can set the size of the individual services—the army, navy, air force, and marines. It can specify the military pay scales, including raises, and it can decide whether military manpower will be acquired through conscription or voluntary enlistment. Much depends on how members of Congress perceive the mood of their constituents. For several years following the Vietnam War, Congress rejected highly visible and expensive Pentagon defense projects, such as the B-1 bomber and an expanded building program for aircraft carriers and submarines, and was very skeptical about the MX missile. The Soviet invasion of Afghanistan in 1979 changed the mood of the public, which, according to opinion surveys, already had begun in the middle 1970s to support increased defense expenditures.[2] Hence, the B-1 bombers are now in production, and an enlarged naval construction program is underway. The development of the MX is making progress; Congress authorized the construction of the first 21 missiles in 1983 after a heated debate. The administration is seeking funds for 40 more missiles, which some members of Congress would like to reduce to 21, while others, such as Representative Joseph P. Addabbo, (D, New York) and chairman of the House Appropriations Subcommittee on Defense, would like to delete all production money from the administration's $5 billion MX request.[3]

Another instrument through which Congress can make its will felt in the defense area is the War Powers Act of 1973, passed over the veto of President Nixon. The purpose of the act was to make the commitment of U.S. armed forces abroad a collective responsibility of the executive and legislative branches. However, under this act, it is Congress that has the final authority in deciding whether or not U.S. forces should be engaged in prolonged military hostilities abroad. It reflects the basic responsibility of Congress to declare war, and, at the same time, it limits the authority of the president to employ the armed forces in his capacity as commander-in-chief. Specifically, according to section 2c of this act, the president may initiate military activity involving hostilities or imminent hostilities only pursuant to a declaration of war, specific statutory authorization, or a national emergency created by an attack upon the United States, its territories or possessions, or its armed services. If the president initiates military activity, he must report his actions to Congress within 48 hours; if possible, he is expected to consult with Congress prior to such action. If Congress does not authorize this activity by legislation or a declaration of war within 60 days, the president must terminate this activity (section 5b). If the president certifies he needs more time for safe withdrawal, Congress may authorize 30 more days. This provision, which allows termination without passage of a bill, circumvents the possibility of a presidential veto. At the same time, it gives the president 90 days to maneuver his forces for the achievement of his objective.

Congress may terminate military activity initiated by the president before the 60-day period by concurrent resolution ordering the immediate withdrawal of the armed forces by the president. Since a concurrent resolution is not subject to the president's signature, no veto is possible.

The question has been raised whether the War Powers Act is an unconstitutional infringement of the president's authority as chief executive and commander-in-chief. During the last 25 to 30 years, presidents have also claimed special authority on the basis of inherent powers.[4]

The constitutionality of the War Powers Act may be tested in the courts, but the outcome is quite uncertain because the issue may be more political than legal, and, therefore, the courts may shy away from a substantive decision. The impact of the 1983 Supreme Court decision severely restricting "legislative vetoes" on the War Powers Act is unclear. But, in any case, it seems that so far the act has not impeded the conduct of foreign policy; indeed, it may have the salutary effect of placing the administration on guard and making it more cautious before undertaking military action. On the other hand, such action was taken when it appeared necessary, although it was not always successful. An example of a successful military action undertaken by a president was the rescue by the marines in 1975 of the *Mayaguez*, a U.S. merchant ship attacked by Cambodian military forces. Unsuccessful military actions include the aborted attempt to free the U.S. hostages in Iran in 1980 and the landings of marines in Lebanon in 1982. As mentioned earlier, strong hostility developed between the president and Congress after the U.S. marines were directly attacked and many killed in Beirut. President Reagan withdrew the troops from Lebanon but blamed Congress for interfering in his foreign policy. During the election year of 1984, more debate on this issue is bound to arise.

ORGANIZATIONAL ASPECTS

Four committees of Congress play a pivotal role in the control over defense spending and the formulation of U.S. defense policy. They are the House and Senate Armed Services committees, and the two Appropriations committees with their subcommittees on Defense. But these are not the only committees concerned with national security. The proliferation of the committee system has led to an estimate by students of Congress that 16 House and 19 Senate committees and an even larger number of subcommittees have an interest in defense and national security and want to have a part of the action.[5] Figure 2.1 lists the defense-related subcommittees of the Senate Appropriations and Armed Services committees.

With the proliferation of the congressional committees has gone a tremendous increase in employees staffing them. During the period from 1955 to 1979, the number increased from just over 5,000 to about 20,000, raising the cost of maintaining the committee staffs from $170 million to $1.2 billion in 1980.[6] Some of these staff members have acquired a high degree of expertise in defense matters, and a few have moved from their congressional jobs to positions in the executive branch. An example is Richard Perle, who was a member of the staff of former Senator Henry Jackson (D, Washington) and is now assistant secretary of defense for international security affairs.

The growth of the committee staffs and the increased expertise in defense matters by some of the staffs have had a number of important consequences. The committees' information-gathering capability relevant to defense policy formulation has been enhanced, and thus their influence over the direction of policy has increased. Networks of communications and coalitions have developed between individual staff members serving representatives and senators and those working for committees. In addition, links have been established between congressional staff members and relevant officials in the Pentagon and the armed services through which important pieces of information and influence might be channeled in both directions.[7] Similar arrangements may also be set up or exist with major lobbyists. Staff members also have a personal interest in their own promotion and therefore

Figure 2.1. Defense-related Senate Committees and Subcommittees

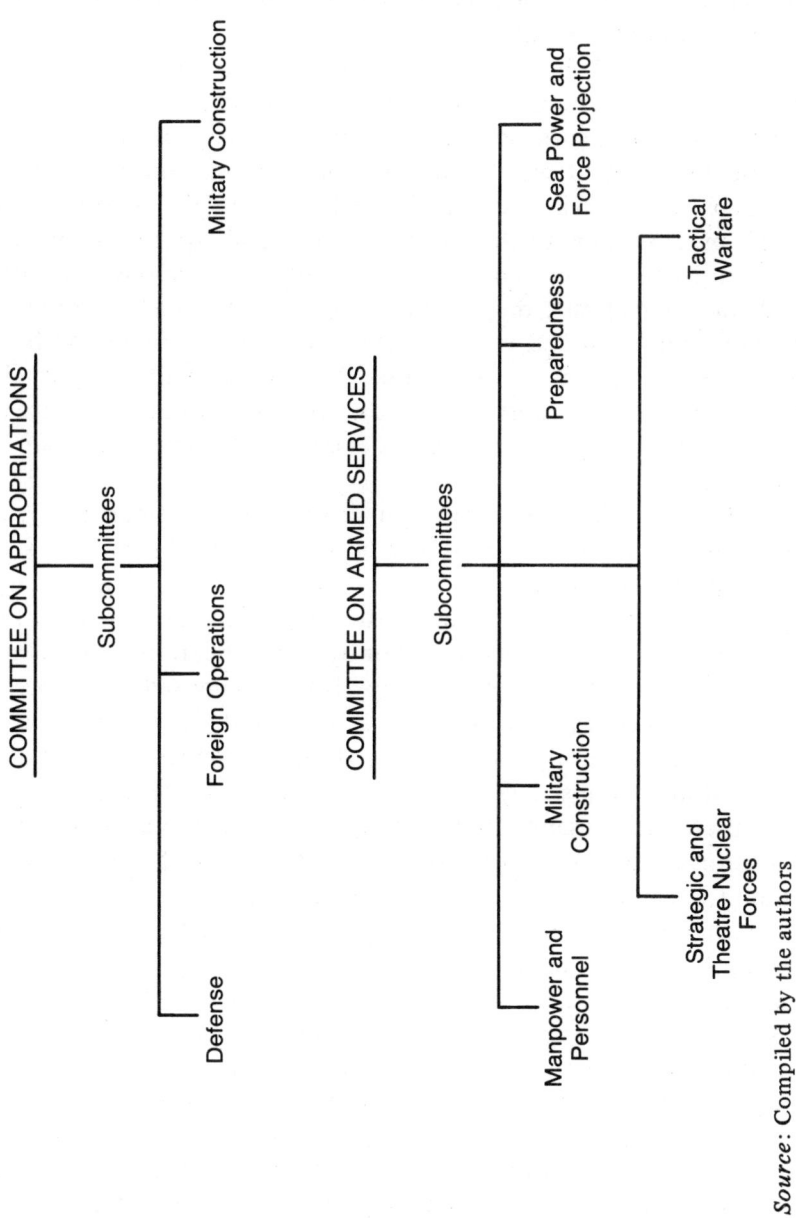

COMMITTEE ON APPROPRIATIONS
Subcommittees
- Defense
- Foreign Operations
- Military Construction

COMMITTEE ON ARMED SERVICES
Subcommittees
- Manpower and Personnel
- Military Construction
- Strategic and Theatre Nuclear Forces
- Preparedness
- Sea Power and Force Projection
- Tactical Warfare

Source: Compiled by the authors

like to see the representative or senator they serve or the committee for which they work become the targets of media attention. Such activities may be rungs on the ladder of power in Washington and at the same time strengthen the overall influence of Congress in the formulation of defense policy.

Because of their influence on defense policy, access to the members of relevant committees is sought by various groups and individuals. For the Pentagon and the armed services, it appears that a strong lobbying effort should have the highest priority. While the secretary of defense and his top-level assistants do indeed regularly make presentations to the Armed Services and Appropriations committees to convince them of the merit of new weapons acquisitions and budget requests, the lobbying activities of industry groups may be more powerful and more effective, as we will see later. As for the efforts of the secretary of defense, they are normally supported by the Joint Chiefs of Staff as far as the Armed Services committees are concerned and by the civilian leadership of the army, navy, and air force.

Alliances of the military with private organizations and groups may produce additional pleas in support of the Pentagon requests for the approval of the proposed budget and acquisition of new weapons systems. They may come from retired high-ranking military officers employed by defense contractors or by public relations firms retained by such contractors. Support may also be expressed by representatives of various think tanks, such as the Rand Corporation, or conservative study groups, such as the Heritage Foundation. But sometimes study groups may also voice opposition to Pentagon requests and therefore present critical analyses of Pentagon aims for the acquisition of new weapons systems. The Center for Defense Information in Washington is an example of such an organization.

Other groups wishing to exert influence on defense policy and to testify before key committees include labor unions and veterans' organizations such as the American Legion, most of which tend to be congenial to increased defense expenditures. At times, even local communities benefiting from defense industries and/or nearby military installations may seek to testify and express their particular viewpoints on defense matters. Finally, individual members of Congress may ask to present their opinions or criticisms on specific aspects of defense before their colleagues sitting on the committees.

Of all the groups seeking to lobby for increased defense expenditures, the most effective and perhaps the most dangerous from the point of view of ensuring a balanced military establishment are large defense contractors. Naturally, each of these wants to promote its own weapons system, and the most profitable systems over a long period of time are those labeled big-ticket: items such as nuclear missiles, fighter planes, bombers, submarines, and aircraft carriers. If a contractor can get a contract for such items, it may corner the market for future generations of that system by making relatively small modifications. Eventually, it may sell obsolete versions of the system overseas to third countries (developed and developing) and do a brisk business in spare parts at very profitable prices.[8]

In view of the considerable economic spread effects of the production of big-ticket items, Congress is often sympathetic to the manufacture of these weapons systems. Indeed, Congress has given the Navy Department almost everything it has requested for its goal of a 600-ship, 15-carrier navy. At the same time, those at the Pentagon are pleased with the award of the large weapons systems because these systems take years to complete and thus bind future budget makers. But, since the United States is not limitless in its financial resources, the emphasis on funding big-ticket items results in neglect for providing funds for the much less "sexy" conventional weapons and for personnel to fight in conventional battles. As a consequence, preparations for conventional war are given lower priorities, and this tends to lower the nuclear flash point at which the United States would resort to nuclear force. More will be said about this issue in later chapters.

THE POLICY-MAKING PROCESS

Foreign policy decision-making analysis suggests that various clusters of variables must be taken into consideration to determine the effective cause or causes of particular policies. These clusters are institutional, idiosyncratic, societal, and international variables.[9] In some cases, variables from different clusters may be relevant; in other cases one or more variables from only one cluster may be decisive. In the formulation of defense policy, it is fair to assume that the Pentagon may be very influential, but, since Congress holds the purse strings, individual representatives and senators, especially those who have acquired expert knowledge in the area of defense, may also inject their particular views on security policy and strategy. Indeed, with Congress having the last word on the defense budget and thus possessing a decisive impact on many aspects of the U.S. military posture, including which weapons may be employed, one would expect a massive lobbying effort on the part of the Defense Department. But, according to Representative Les Aspin (D, Wisconsin), this is not the case. "Actually, the Defense Department doesn't lobby as much as popular perception would have it. Essentially, the Defense Department relies on three pre-existing and permanent factors to forward its cause—jobs, an appeal to emotion, and a monopoly on expertise."[10] Each major weapons program carries with it the promise of increased employment in several congressional districts. Hence, the Pentagon knows that it can count on several members of Congress to be on the DOD's side since jobs for their constituents are always of the utmost importance for those politicians who want to stay in Congress. Aspin goes on to say, "If the navy wanted to shut me up, it could do so ever so effectively by assigning a fleet to Racine, Wisconsin."[11]

The appeal to emotion is not difficult to carry out. Americans in general are very patriotic, and members of Congress do not want to be accused of being responsible for making the United States vulnerable to potential enemy forces. As Aspin remarks, "The biggest emotional kick . . . comes from the periodic revelations of growing Soviet military prowess. The Pentagon feeds the image of the Russian bear as ten feet tall. Each new weapon proposed by the Pentagon is necessary, therefore, to meet the threat posed by some new Russian advancement. . . .The Russians do conveniently help the Pentagon sell its programs. All the Pentagon has to do is package the announcements in the most dramatic way."[12]

Of course, this technique is not unique to the Pentagon. The Soviet military establishment uses U.S. buildups in weapons and men as leverage on the civilians in the Politburo to expand the Soviet armed forces and, since the Communist Party hierarchy depends to a much greater degree on the goodwill of the generals and admirals to maintain its position of power than is the case with the civilian leadership in the United States, the Soviet military is able to impose its will with relative ease when it comes to weapons procurement.

Finally, the Department of Defense relies on its expertise in the highly complex field of strategy and weapons to press for the acceptance of its proposals. This is a good bet because only members of Congress sitting on defense-related committees and subcommittees learn much about weaponry, and some of those, who are reserve officers of high rank such as Senator Barry Goldwater, are convinced supporters of the armed forces anyway.

But there are also critics who have gained expertise in DOD procurement procedures, the capabilities and vulnerabilities of weapons systems, and the intricacies of global and regional strategy. They are able to debate weapons and defense policy and their voices are heard and respected. However, how far they can influence Congress to defeat proposals by the Pentagon in major weapons systems remains to be seen. Unless they have powerful allies in the executive, mainly the president, as for example in the B-1 contest under President Carter, Congress may not do much more than nibble on defense budgets. What reductions are made usually are in noncritical areas or are cosmetic. A study by the Library of Congress for the fiscal years from 1971 to 1976 showed that 6.3 percent of the cumulative Pentagon requests were cut, but an analysis of these cuts indicated that only 2 percent of reductions could actually affect defense policy. The pertinent parts of this study are quoted by Aspin.

1. Nine percent of the cuts were in noncritical areas such as reductions in servants for generals, in the number of public relations men at the Pentagon, and in funds for the construction of new commissaries.
2. Thirty-five percent were illusory cuts or simply financial adjustments, such as the elimination of aid for South Vietnam after Saigon had fallen and of funds that the services had testified were no longer needed because of changed circumstances.
3. Twenty percent were not cuts but postponements; for example, if a program was experiencing development difficulties, Congress dropped funds for procurement until the problems were resolved.
4. The remaining 36 percent of the cuts (or just 2 percent of the total requests) were in areas that could actually affect defense policy.[13]

One problem for congressional decision makers is that mail from constituents is likely to espouse opposing positions. This was the case when in the fall of 1979 the House of Representatives was called upon to vote on the resumption of peacetime Selective Service registration. It was strongly opposed by liberal groups and college students but considered essential by conservatives and those who considered U.S. national security to be deficient. A similar dilemma for members of Congress arose when the B-1 bomber became a front-burner issue. One means frequently used by representatives to overcome this dilemma and to give a somewhat satisfactory response to those constituents whose demands on national security issues were not accommodated is to claim that "procedure" made a favorable vote unattainable.

Agreement on procedural rules for important votes is easier to obtain in Congress than on some highly controversial issues. Once procedural rules have been agreed upon, constraints are imposed on congressional voting behavior, and this allows members of Congress to mask many of their votes and often their true feelings about an issue from their constituents.

Procedure can also be utilized by Congress to defy the wishes of the executive without engaging in outright confrontation. An example of this strategy is provided by David Halbertstein in his book *The Best and the Brightest*.[14] When the question arose about possible U.S. military intervention in Indochina during 1954, President Eisenhower attempted to get a joint resolution of Congress authorizing the employment of naval and air forces to save the French who were besieged at Dien-bien Phu. Lyndon Johnson, then Senate majority leader, was reluctant about the adoption of such a resolution because it would saddle Congress with the responsibility for another possible war while Korea was still fresh in the minds of the American people. At the same time, Johnson did not want to be accused personally, and he did not want the Democrats to be accused collectively, of denying the president the means to resist communist expansion and thus to be blamed for losing Indochina. To solve this dilemma, Johnson injected a series of procedural hurdles in the form of questions to Secretary of State John Foster Dulles during a two-hour meeting. Did the United States have allies who would put up sizable numbers of troops, air force personnel, and naval resources? Had Dulles consulted with any allies? This had not been done.

> By the time the two-hour meeting was over, Johnson had exposed the frailty of the administration's position. (This may have been exactly what Eisenhower wanted, to expose his case and have the Congress itself pick apart the weaknesses. Eisenhower was a subtle man, and no fool, though in pursuit of his objectives he did not like to be thought of as brilliant; people of brilliance, he thought, were distrusted. It was not by chance that he had not been present; let Dulles make the case.) The military were far from unanimous about whether to undertake the air strike. In addition, the United States might have to go it alone if it entered a ground war. Dulles was told to sign up allies, though it was known that Anthony Eden was dubious. Thus the burden, which the administration had ever so gently been trying to shift to the Congress, had now been ever so gently shifted back, if not to the administration, at least to the British, who were known to be unenthusiastic.[15]

Procedure, thus, can be utilized by Congress to avoid direct responsibility. Members of Congress are able to mask their votes by invoking procedure and achieve their objectives without undue confrontation with the executive while at the same time protecting themselves politically.

Procedural rules designed to restrict executive freedom of action can also be introduced through legislation. First, organizations can be established to carry out certain functions with relative independence or to submit periodic reports to congressional committees. A second procedural device is to require certain findings before specific programs can be carried out. For example, certain foreign aid activities can be undertaken only after progress in human rights in the recipient country has been certified. Third, Congress can designate specific government officials to make particular decisions. For example, the act establishing the naval petroleum reserve requires that any decision to release petroleum from it has to be approved by the secretary of the navy.[16] Finally, Congress can designate itself to make the ultimate decision. An example is the War Powers Act, which makes Congress the final arbiter of whether troops should be used. But how forcefully Congress is likely to exercise this authority is not yet clear. The resolution of Congress passed in September 1983 giving President Reagan eighteen months for keeping U.S. marines in Lebanon as a peace-keeping force may reflect less the power of Congress under this act than the political skill of the president in circumventing the restrictions embodied in this legislation.

Ripley and Franklin distinguish three types of foreign and defense policies in accordance with the kind of policy surrounding each. The three types are referred to as structural, strategic, and crisis policy.[17]

Structural Policy

The characteristics of structural policy are regarded as virtually the same as for domestic distributive policy, which is based on the typology of and involves actors from subcommittees and small units in the private sector (individuals, corporations, interest groups) who dominate policy making on the basis of mutual noninterference and logrolling. The implementation of these policy decisions takes place in decentralized fashion.

The decisions reached within the structural policy context are not likely to be changed in subsequent stages of the formal legislative process. The reason is the high level of cooperation between representatives and civil servants because both groups are highly motivated to serve their clients, who are frequently the same individuals or groups. Differences of views are often reconciled by the issue-interested circle of participants involved in a policy-making process. Efforts are made not to expand the number of participants and to prevent outsiders such as the secretary of defense or a congressional party leader from intervening.[18]

Examples of structural policy matters are ongoing procurement requests for weapons, equipment, and manpower. But participants in structural policy making—subcommittees, middle-range DOD bureaucrats, and lobbyists for interest groups and defense contractors—are also influential when it comes to the adoption of new weapons systems such as the B-1.[19] An extensive liaison framework set up between the Department of Defense and the congressional committee system employing a very large staff of DOD officers and civilians strengthens cooperation on structural policy items and in general helps the adoption of defense budget requests and of supporting foreign policies desired by the administration.

A very recent example of structural policy making, which also reflects congressional concerns with jobs, is the debate in the Senate regarding the number of M-1 tanks to be purchased for the army. The Pentagon had requested annual production of 720 of these tanks, whose quality was highly controversial, but the Armed Services Committee and the Appropriations Committee had voted to increase the number to 840, and the committee reports to the full Senate for the 1984 defense budget included this figure. Senator Stevens (R, Alaska), the majority whip, proposed an amendment on November 3, 1983 to bring the number of M-1 tanks to be procured back to 720, especially since this figure continued to be the DOD's target although, understandably, the army would have been pleased to have the larger number. In the Senate debate Senator Stevens asserted that "the decision to go to 840 is an economic decision, it is not a military decision."[20] However, several senators, some of whom had a stake in increasing the number of jobs in their states as a result of the larger number of tanks to be produced, fought hard to stick with 840. These senators, including Levin (D, Michigan), Johnston (D, Louisiana), and Huddleston (D, Kentucky), advanced emotional and "money-saving" arguments (the more tanks are procured, the lower the unit cost) to persuade the Senate to approve the figure of 840. Senator Stevens characterized these efforts correctly when he said:

Anybody with any sense will look around and see we have people—with due respect to my colleagues from Kentucky, from Louisiana, from Michigan—all over the country involved in the M-1 tank now. It has a constituency of its own and it is growing. It is going to be hard to keep this production even at the level of 840 if it keeps up. . . .

There is no convincing military reason that has been advanced here for 840 tanks. Again, we may not have the engines, we will not have the Bradley fighting vehicles to go along with them. There is no reason to roll off those 840 tanks. We should keep that production at the current efficient rate of production which is 720. . . .

But this is a test. This is going to fall on the ears of the American public, by the people who are going to increase the number of tanks solely for economic reasons, in terms of jobs in certain localities in the country. We could spend our way into oblivion that way.

It is not right to increase the rate of production of a very significant portion of the Department's arsenal beyond what they have requested. We will still produce, if my amendment is adopted, 120 more tanks a year than the Bradley fighting vehicle. Two years later we can produce the same number of tanks and will not have to borrow the money long in advance to produce them.

I knew what I was doing when I brought this up, because I want people to think; and I think the Senate should think before we face these other amendments.

How many people are now going to increase the budget for defense over and above the President's request, just for the purpose of producing 120 more tanks per year in order to have a jobs program out of the Department of Defense?[21]

Senator Stevens did not prevail. The politics of reelection caused the senators opposed to the amendment to carry the day.

Strategic Policy

In strategic policy matters, the role of subcommittees, middle-range bureaucrats, and interest groups (corporations) is reduced and the main decision-making locus shifts to top-level actors in the executive branch and Congress. The implementation of decisions is usually centralized, with the National Security Council playing an important part. Strategy policy decisions occur in noncrisis as well as crisis situations.

The issues for strategic policies may involve new weapons systems (the MX or the B-1) and, as noted with respect to the B-1, in such instances the structural policy interaction framework may be active as well. However, the final decision is likely to be made at the highest level of government. But strategic policy may also pertain to major trade issues and sanctions vis-à-vis the Soviet Union, economic and military aid to allies, and the posture and quantity of U.S. forces abroad.

U.S. trade with the Soviet Union has been an issue before Congress on several occasions since World War II. The desire of President Nixon and Secretary of State Kissinger in 1973 and 1974 to expand this trade ran into rough weather in Congress, which wanted to link expansion to Soviet authorization for increased emigration of Jews from the USSR to Israel. And, indeed, Congress succeeded in this effort when it adopted an amendment to pending international trade legislation that had been prepared by Senator Henry Jackson (D, Washington). The problem of various restrictions on U.S. exports to the Soviet Union—the Carter grain embargo in 1980 and its lifting by Reagan in 1981, as well as an imposition of sanctions on the delivery of parts for the Soviet-West European natural gas pipeline by Reagan, come to mind—also aroused heated debates in Congress and in some of its committees, where opposition to administration policies surfaced with varying force.

U.S. aid to two major NATO allies became the object of a major dispute in Congress during the middle 1970s as a result of the Turkish invasion of the island of Cyprus, which was strongly resented by Greece. Strong pressures by Americans of Greek extraction on Congress led eventually (February 1975) to a cutoff of military aid to Turkey. It was not until 1978 that President Carter, labeling the repeal of the cutoff his number one foreign policy priority, succeeded in restoring aid to Turkey. To achieve this success required his personal lobbying of members of the House and Senate as well as personal intervention by the then NATO commander, Alexander Haig, and the secretaries of state and defense. Some of the top leaders of Congress also aided in the endeavor. To obtain final consent from Congress, the president had to certify that resumption of aid was "in the national interest of the United States and the interest of NATO"; moreover, he had to certify that Turkey was acting in good faith in settling a number of Cyprus-related issues.[22] As Ripley and Franklin point out, "decisions in congressional committees had no finality—final decisions were made on the floors of the House and Senate after heated debates. Those decisions required compromise that left Congress with the illusion of being important in continued decision making on this subject, and the president got the essence of what he wanted."[23] Similar considerations also apply to aid to El Salvador in the early 1980s. The Reagan administration's policy of emphasizing military aid aroused much controversy in Congress, where many members wanted to reduce military assistance in favor of greater economic aid and where claims of human rights violations by the Salvadoran armed forces brought forth calls for a complete cutoff of military support. In these controversies, subcommittee chairmen played initiating roles, but final decisions were influenced strongly by top-level actors in Congress and the executive, including President Reagan.

Another aspect of strategic policy has been reflected in controversies about the numbers of U.S. troops in foreign countries. Congress successfully insisted on the withdrawal of all U.S. forces from Vietnam in the middle 1970s, but it failed to compel the reduction of U.S. troops in Europe in spite of efforts by then Senate Majority Leader Mike Mansfield, who worked on this for several years until he retired from Congress in 1976. It should be noted that the House Armed Services Committee had recommended against unilateral troop withdrawal from Europe.

While the foregoing discussion suggests that in strategic policy issues the influence of top-level actors in the executive and Congress as a whole is likely to carry the day with respect to the final decisions taken, competing points of view expressed by members of Congress who are recognized experts in various defense fields may well be listened to with greater attention than when it comes to structural policy issues. Since decisions on the latter issues are bargained out in most cases on a lower level and officers, if possible, are kept out of the limelight, inputs by congressional defense experts may not be sought nor may these experts be sufficiently interested to offer their counsel. However, no hard and fast rule can be established because some issues such as the B-1 could well be considered as much a strategic policy issue as a structural policy one.

Crisis Policy

Crisis policies regarding foreign and defense situations are formulated by the president in consultation with only a few top advisers, perhaps a few leading individual members of Congress, and sometimes leaders of relevant nongovernmental groups. "The issues are defined quickly, debated in private by the executive actors, and responded to quickly in a highly centralized fashion through executive (presidential) action."[24] However, the decisions taken may generate considerable public debate and maybe opposition. Controversy between the executive and Congress may develop after policy implementation and may lead to congressional resolutions either supporting or opposing the presidential action. However, subcommittee interaction with middle-rank officials of executive departments does not play a role in this policy-making process and "generally, the presidential view of issues left in controversy prevails in one way or another."[25]

The best example of crisis policy formulation is the Cuban missile crisis of 1962, when President Kennedy consulted only a very small number of close advisers, including his brother Robert, Theodore Sorenson, and the secretaries of state and defense. The decision, made within six days, was to impose a naval quarantine on Soviet missile shipments to Cuba and to demand that existing bases and missiles be dismantled and returned to the Soviet Union.[26] Prior to announcing the quarantine decision, Kennedy met with leaders of Congress to inform them of what was planned. Interestingly, many congressmen were highly critical and, in emotional terms, expressed the view that more forceful action should be taken, including a military attack, and that the blockade was far too weak.[27] However, in this situation the president's decision proved to be correct.

Another example of crisis policy making took place in 1975 when the U.S. merchant ship *Mayaguez* was seized by Cambodia, which claimed that the ship was in its waters, while Washington insisted it was in international waters. President Ford decided to employ marines to rescue the ship; no consultation under the War Powers Act took place. The 1979 seizure of the U.S. embassy in Iran could also fall into the category of a crisis situation, but the decision to attempt a major operation for the rescue of the U.S. hostages was not made until several months after the hostages were seized. In this case, the application of the War Powers Act could require no more than that the president inform Congress after the fact. Indeed, in fast-moving crisis situations Congress may not be able to do much more than endorse the president's action or voice ex post facto complaints.

This chapter has given us general insights into congressional involvement in policy making on national defense and related matters. We will now proceed to an examination of particular issues related broadly to nuclear warfare in which congressional experts have offered solutions. We will begin our discussion with the problems surrounding strategic weapons, to be followed by those raised in the controversy about theater nuclear weapons and alliance policy.

Finally, we will look at selected Third World problems, particularly the Middle East and Central America, as they may affect U.S. nuclear weapons strategies.

NOTES

1. Cecil V. Crabb, Jr., *American Foreign Policy in the Nuclear Age*, 4th ed. (New York: Harper & Row, 1983), p. 199.

2. Werner J. Feld and John K. Wildgen, *NATO and the Atlantic Defense* (New York: Praeger, 1982), p. 79.

3. *International Herald Tribune*, March 14, 1984.

4. Duane Lockard, *The Perverted Priorities of American Politics* (New York: Macmillan, 1971), pp. 234-37.

5. Amos A. Jordan and William J. Taylor, Jr., *American National Security* (Baltimore, Md.: The Johns Hopkins University Press, 1981), p. 112. As far as foreign policy in general is concerned, over 50 subcommittees in the House alone are supposed to be actively involved in some aspect of such policy (Cecil V. Crabb, Jr., and Pat M. Holt, *Invitation to Struggle*. Washington, D.C.: Congressional Quarterly Press, 1980).

6. Crabb, *American Foreign Policy*, pp. 218-19.

7. See Randall B. Ripley and Grace A. Franklin, *Congress, the Bureaucracy, and Public Policy* (Homewood, Ill.: Dorsey Press, 1980), pp. 54-55.

8. Amitai Etzioni, "Lobbyists can be Disarming," *International Herald Tribune*, April 19, 1984, p. 4.

9. See Werner J. Feld, *American Foreign Policy: Aspirations and Reality* (New York: John Wiley, 1984), pp. 17-134.

10. Les Aspin, "Congress Against the Defense Department," in *The Tethered Presidency*, edited by Thomas M. Franck (New York: New York University Press, 1981), pp. 245-63, on p. 245.

11. Ibid.

12. Ibid., p. 246.

13. Ibid., pp. 248-49.

14. David Halberstein, *The Best and the Brightest* (New York: Random House, 1973), pp. 140-44.

15. Ibid., p. 141.

16. Aspin, "Congress Against the Defense Department," p. 259.

17. Ripley and Franklin, *Congress, the Bureaucracy, and Public Policy*, pp. 184-85.

18. Ibid., p. 185.

19. For details, see ibid., pp. 191-95.

20. *Congressional Record*, Vol. 129, No. 149, November 3, 1983, p. S15337.

21. Ibid., pp. S15339 and S15341.

22. Ripley and Franklin, *Congress, the Bureaucracy, and Public Policy*, pp. 203-4.

23. Ibid., p. 203.

24. Ibid., p. 185.

25. Ibid., p. 186.

26. For a detailed analysis of how this decision was made, see Graham T. Allison, *Essence of Decision: Explaining the Cuban Missile Crisis* (Boston: Little, Brown, 1971).

27. Robert F. Kennedy, *Thirteen Days* (New York: Norton, 1981), pp. 31-32.

3
MAJOR CONGRESSIONAL VIEWS ON STRATEGIC WEAPONS SYSTEMS: THE UNTHINKABLE CONGRESS MUST PONDER

IMPOSING ORDER ON CHAOS

As we have seen in previous chapters, members of Congress do not all see themselves, or their branch of government, as fully involved as they might be in the development of U.S. strategic policy. To a certain extent, this is an unavoidable and irresolvable argument in a constitutional framework that puts so much emphasis on separation of powers. Overall, we think it is fair to say that Congress largely has to react to Pentagon and presidential initiatives in military policy. Congressional initiates are rather rare—but not unheard of.

Summarizing executive branch's strategic initiatives is not easy. No one can suggest that there is a lack of documentation; the problem is that there is too much—and most of the surfeit of material is couched in carefully blurred terms. To borrow an analogy from communications theory, there is a very low signal to noise ratio in U.S. strategic statements. Not all of this ambiguity is deliberate Orwellian doublespeak or doublethink; some of it is an outgrowth of the inherent difficulty we have in thinking about thermonuclear war. Fred Kaplan's concluding remarks in his study of the Rand Corporation, from its inception following World War II through the early 1980s, captures the difficulty eloquently. "The nuclear strategists had come to impose order—but in the end, chaos still prevailed."[1]

Kaplan's views of this strain of U.S. intellectual history seem unassailable. As a result, one has to have a high tolerance for hedging on the part of politicians' attempts to explain strategic policy. Still, there is some pattern to the chaos of nuclear strategy—even though the order in that pattern may be artificial. The pattern in the chaos the members of Congress have to deal with daily is one we can think of as imposed by the administration. It provides us with a point of departure.

REAGAN'S STRATEGIC MAP

The Reagan administration's point of departure has had a long prologue; there is nothing truly innovative in the intellectual baggage either President Reagan or his important advisors bring to strategic policy making. Many of his ideas have been popular among Republicans and conservative Democrats, the kinds of people who formed groups such as the Committee on the Present Danger. One of the most concise and revealing statements of how Reagan has synthesized a great many ideas comes from his announcement on October 2, 1981 of his strategic weapons program.[2] During the campaign in the almost two years preceding this statement, U.S. voters, even unalert and inattentive voters, had had ample opportunity to learn that one of Reagan's major differences with Carter was over strategic weaponry. The October 1981 announcement was another installment in repaying campaign promises.

The Reagan plan had five major points for the public and Congress to ponder. His first point, chronologically, was an announcement that he planned to deploy 100 B-1 bombers. This was a turnaround from a Carter decision to drop the B-1. (Carter chose to pursue a new generation of bomber technology commonly called "stealth," after its assorted properties that resist detection by Soviet air self-defense forces. This was not announced until well into the campaign. But we have found no evidence that Carter had a specific aircraft on the drawing board.) Reagan's second point was the decision to use a "steady rate" of Trident submarine acquisition. Along with deployment of these sophisticated boats, Reagan also announced a follow-on missile for the Trident's current C-4 projectile, the D-5. The third point was a decision to deploy MX missiles in existing Minuteman silos while still pursuing "three promising long-term options for basing the MX missile" prior to full depolyment.[3] Reagan's fourth point was a major effort in command and communications. This is an area where U.S. military experts seem to feel quite vulnerable. Any threat to the communication of orders to or from the battlefield (presumably a nuclear one), from the president's person down to the smallest silicon chip, is an obvious limit to the credibility of any U.S. deterrent. His fifth and final point was a reference to the idea of strategic defense, never strongly emphasized in the United States since the fervid bomb shelter activities of the 1950s. Included here were allusions to improved surveillance, air defense, and closer ties with Canada.

As enunciated in terms of the above paragraph, the Reagan program appears to be largely a weapons system program that marks a sharp departure from the Carter path. This greatly simplifies congressional speaking on any president's strategic program; weapons systems are great windmills and Reagan made clear the difference between Reagan windmills and Carter windmills.

THE RATIONALE BEHIND THE SHOPPING LIST

Even though both Reagan and his critics liked to call the five items described above the "Reagan strategic package," his shopping list had been around for some time; there was nothing essentially new in it in terms of either actual systems or their role in U.S. defense posture. Reagan's own opening remarks noted that his plan would "strengthen and modernize the strategic triad of land-based missiles, sea-based missiles, and bombers."[4]

The notion of the triad, that is, the three generic types of U.S. strategic weapons, has been rather much an article of faith within the defense community. While a few call for reliance on a diad (that is, dropping land-based missiles because of their vulnerability and using only bombers and submarines), it is also possible to move to a strategic quartet. "In the early 1980s, it will be possible to add a new element—the long-range cruise missile."[5]

The basic motives behind a triad, or any multimodal approach to strategic weapons, are almost intuitively obvious. One obtains redundancy, targeting flexibility, and complicates technological countermeasures and attack tactics by the adversary. This strengthens deterrence. Individual weapons systems within a diad, triad, or whatever, are still open to charges of hampering crisis stability. Reagan went on in his statement to list some specific goals for his package: enhancing

Figure 3.1. Nuclear Budget Breakdown

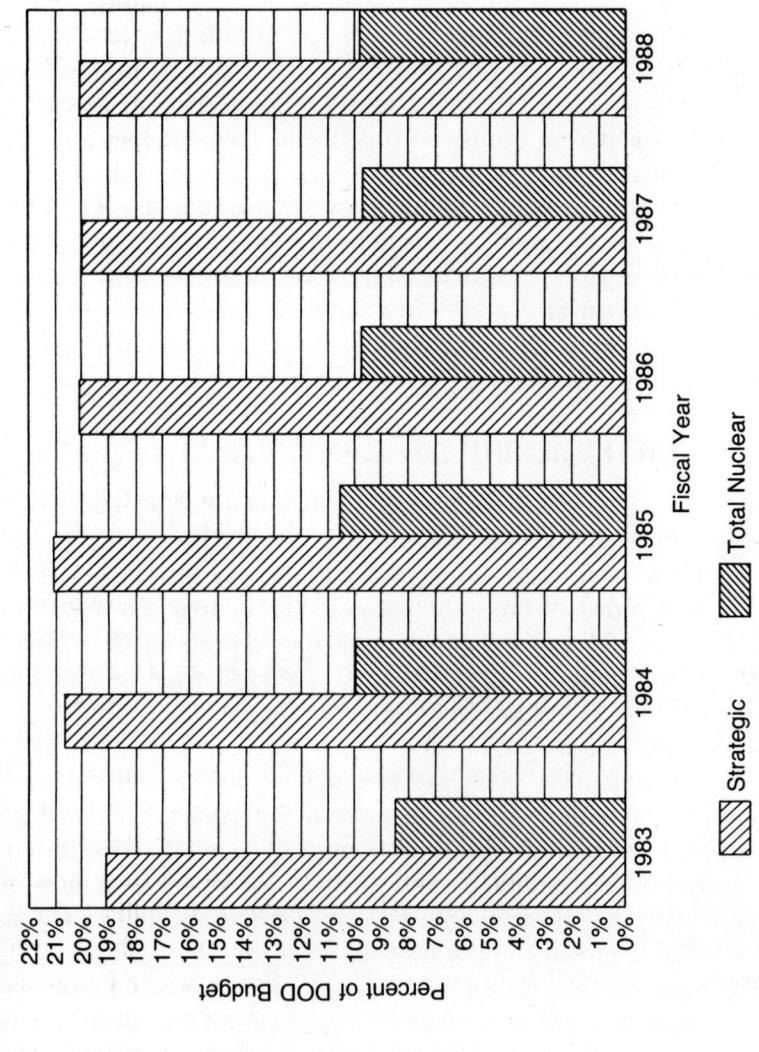

Source: Department of Defense, Report of the Secretary of Defense, 1984.

both deterrence and our notion of "extended deterrence," response at reasonable cost to the growth of Soviet forces, and the arms control implications of a signal to the USSR that the United States is willing to acquire arms at a pace matching any moves they might make. Again, there was nothing innovative here in terms of long-term doctrine. What was new was Reagan's obvious determination to push ahead with familiar programs that previous administrations had eschewed. To some extent, we can quantitatively grasp the amount of strategic innovation in Reagan's planning by referring to figure 3.1, which shows projected proportions of the defense budget allocated to all nuclear forces and to strategic nuclear forces; the direction of change is not apparent, and the amount of change appears minimal.

SOME ILLUSTRATIVE CONGRESSIONAL VIEWS

Reaction to Reagan's package in Congress largely concentrated on three issues: cost, familiar weapons like the B-1 or MX, and futuristic alternatives to the concept of deterrence. Representative Joseph P. Addabbo's remarks to the House Committee on Appropriations are instructive in that they show one kind of thinking a visible congressional defense expert employs. Addabbo had advocated a cut of $11.2 billion in defense appropriations, $2.4 billion of which he would have taken from the B-1 bomber. "Almost all of the bad things that can happen to a major procurement program are present in the B-1 bomber program. There is far too much concurrency between development and production. More than one half of the aircraft are scheduled to be produced and delivered before the development program has been completed. The B1-B is obsolete. It is an old design. There are better ways to penetrate enemy defenses than those offered by the B1-B. The costs are completely out of control."[6] Addabbo turned to the MX, about which he noted, "I strongly disagree with the decision by the Committee, by a vote of 25 to 23, to reverse the decision of the Defense Subcommittee to provide 1.9 billion for the MX. Following cancellation by the Administration of the Multiple Protective Shelter system, we held special hearings on the President's so-called "strategic package." We received testimony from the Secretary of Defense and his deputies, and from Air Force personnel. One thing came through very clearly—the basing mode of the MX is now completely unknown."[7] The bulk of Addabbo's comments went into another major consideration often found in Congress, the issues of cost, waste, mismanagement, and diversion of funds from pressing domestic programs. His statement ended with the comment, "We must use the role of reason and keep defense spending under control and not sacrifice many genuine needs of our people needlessly."[8]

Addabbo's arguments find echoes in the views of Colorado's Representative Patricia Schroeder, who has, like Addabbo, demonstrated an interest in defense without acquiring, yet, a reputation as a full-fledged defense-oriented member of Congress. In remarks made in April 1982, Schroeder emphasized cost concerns, as did Addabbo some months earlier. She singled out a number of programs she felt especially noteworthy, including additional carriers, the B-1, the MX, chemical weapons, and civil defense. She also wrote that "the authorization bill passed by this body demonstrates a disregard of the national public outcry for a freeze on the production and deployment of nuclear weapons."[9]

The remarks of Representatives Addabbo and Schroeder fall into a generic classification: guns versus butter. Even though the remarks above may criticize the technical merits of a particular weapons system, the basis of the criticism is not essentially military, especially not strategic. A contrasting set of reactions on the House side can be found in the remarks of Ronald V. Dellums from California. There is no gainsaying Dellums's concerns about the economic implications of defense spending. His views on the economic implications of arms costs were clear even before the announcement of Reagan's strategic package. In May 1981 Dellums wrote, "We are financing an increase in the military budget in a manner that is the least politically risky and the safest way to do it. Levying taxes has political implications; engaging in continued budget deficits has political implications, but ripping off the poor, ripping off working-class people, ripping off senior citizens, ripping off the children and middle income citizens of America is becoming the safest way to engage in financing military budgets."[10] Cost arguments such as these are complex; they also can be complicated by the use of varying standards of measurement. For example, figures 3.2 and 3.3 apparently show the same information—authorized military spending over a series of years. But figure 3.2, with its dramatic steep slope, is based on current dollars. That is, 1952 dollars are compared with dollars in subsequent years with no control for inflation. Figure 3.3, on the other hand, suggests a decline in defense spending based on constant dollars, in which inflation is taken into account. What needs to be observed is that 1952 was a war year while 1983 was not. Statistical presentations such as the ones these figures were derived from abound in government documents. They do not contribute to the clarity of argument.

Figure 3.2. Total Obligational Authority, History and Projection

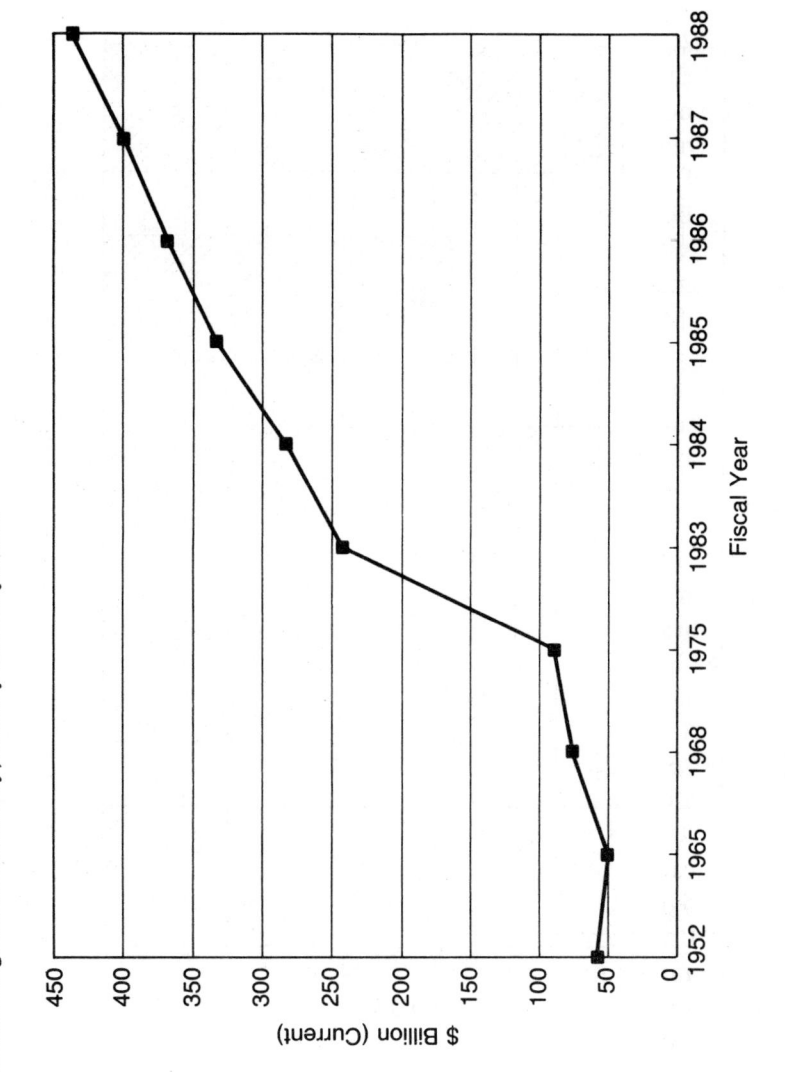

Source: Adapted from Report of the Secretary of Defense, 1984.

Figure 3.3. Total Obligational Authority, Constant 1984 Dollars

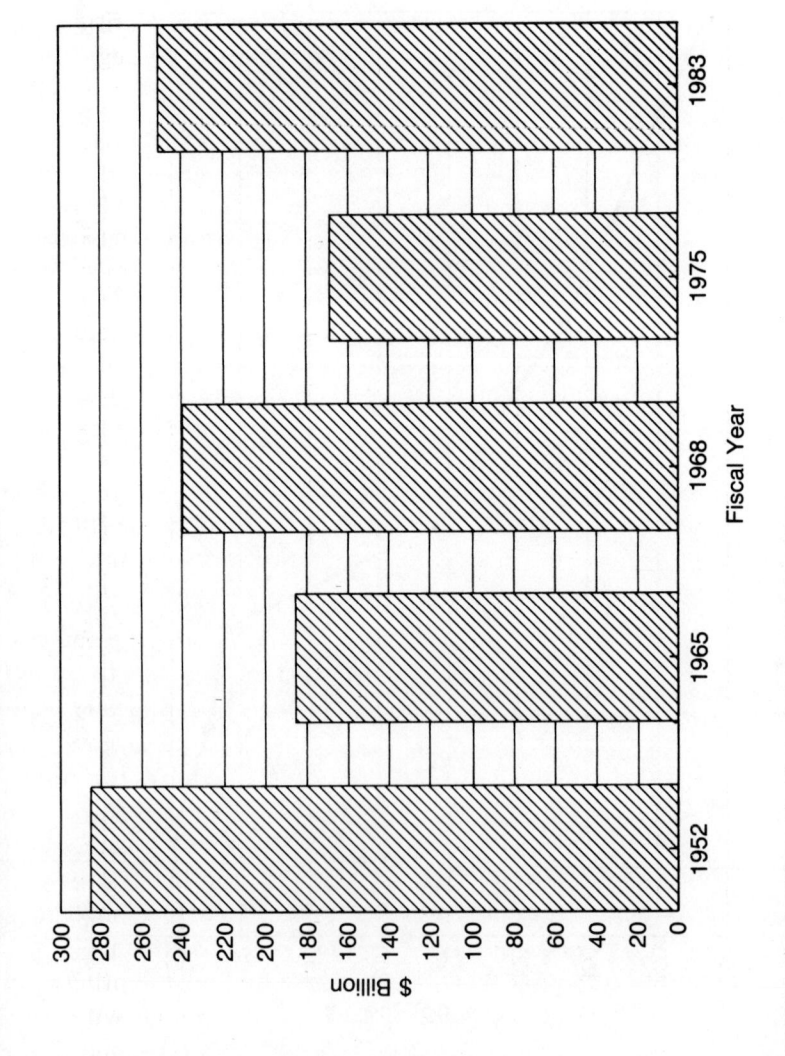

Source: Adapted from The Annual Report of the Secretary of Defense, 1984.

It can be easily granted that Dellums's use of the language is remarkably explicit for an elected official; he is just plain more blunt than Addabbo or Schroeder, for example. But where he differs is not just in style but in actual content. His statements contain military arguments that need to be taken seriously, whether they are correct or not from a technical point of view. After all, he does have the prerogatives of a member of Congress. Dellums has a critique of virtually every major U.S. weapons program and the strategic rationale behind it. Let us take some of his comments verbatim.

> The Administration correctly decided to abandon the MPS basing mode realizing that without a SALT II treaty the Soviets could certainly deploy enough warheads to saturate each shelter. Although the Administration has not decided on a permanent basing mode for this missile, the Committee has authorized over $3,700 million [sic] for this weapons system. The rationale for the MX has been that the nation needs a "survivable" land-based missile that also has counterforce capability. However, no survivable basing mode has been accepted. If the MX is placed in fixed silos; if the plan to harden the silos is unworkable; and if our missiles and theirs are not as accurate as we have been led to believe, since no testing north-south has ever been tried, then why build this expensive, yet unnecessary weapon? Also, if they are as accurate as their proponents claim, then they pose a different danger attendant to their deployment—launch on warning by the Soviets. Further, the MX will be crisis destabilizing, thereby degrading our national security.[11]

In this critique, other than the reference to the cost, we see genuine military objections to the MX—even though they are to an extent mutually exclusive. Dellums suggests that the MX, basically, will not work—a good enough reason to abandon it. But, he suggests, even if it will work it will be "crisis destabilizing, thereby degrading our national security."

Crisis destabilization is a strategic concept that basically says that weapons can become too usable. That is, by their being structured in a way that makes them vulnerable, for example, any ongoing crisis puts an adversary in a position of "use them or lose them."

Equally crisis destabilizing are weapons that are tempting to strike because of a high military value. For example, a missile with ten warheads is obviously more tempting than one with only one warhead. Most crisis unstable is a vulnerably based MIRVed missile or other weapon system. The MX is obviously in this category.

We do not intend to answer Dellums here—that is not our mission. Still, it needs to be pointed out that part of the strategic rationale for the MX is precisely its crisis instability. The United States has a great problem assuring the credibility of its extended deterrence—its nuclear guarantee to allies in Western Europe. Crisis stable weapons do not reassure them of our willingness to employ a nuclear response. Once Europeans are under Soviet attack, U.S. crisis stability becomes U.S. unreliability—unwillingness to engage the USSR in their defense. One of the properties that makes the MX's vice of crisis instability a virtue of usability lies in the counterforce properties Dellums mentions. These properties have a peculiar reassuring effect on notions of extended deterrence. The concept of counterforce, a Rand Corporation buzzword meaning that the weapon is designed to hit hardened military targets rather than soft cities (targeted by countercity or countervalue weapons), suggests that weapons are designed to be used against other weapons. This may mean missiles in silos. It may, in addition, mean hardened command, control, communications, and intelligence centers or other targets essential to maintaining an assault. Counterforce weapons with the projected capabilities of the MX promise this "assault-breaking" capability. Some strategists think this a more credible extended deterrent than a countervalue extended deterrent, in which we could bomb Smolensk in retaliation for an assault on Frankfurt, thus risking an attack on New York. It would be better, more credible, some argue, to threaten Byelorussian command centers with the MX, thus sparing Soviet cities and encouraging them to spare European and U.S. cities, while still hampering the progress of Soviet armed forces across the European plain.

There is a real difficulty in this line of thinking. First, we agree with Kaplan that it is chaotic. There is no appeal in common sense to counterforce with its implications of "war fighting" and limited nuclear wars. Dellums argues:

> Nuclear weapons can only be used for deterrence. The architect of "deterrence," former Secretary of Defense McNamara, argued that if we could, in retaliation, assure unacceptance [sic] destruction of the population and economy of our adversary, then we could deter any first attack. We unequivocally have that capacity. Talk of limited nuclear strikes, surgical strikes, and theater nuclear exchanges is a flight of fantasy. In fact, any engagement between the major adversaries at all, must be assumed to result in total nuclear war. We must turn from confrontation to negotiation.[12]

This, of course, puts the shoe quite on the other foot. Some readers may find an irony in seeing a liberal cite Robert McNamara on military matters. He was the architect, in the view of many liberals, of the Vietnam War as well as of a (but not the only) deterrence doctrine. It is called mutual assured destruction (MAD). It has the same level of intuitive appeal as does counterforce. Counterforce asks us to believe in deterrence based on limited or controllable nuclear exchanges; MAD asks us to believe in deterrence based on mutual suicide.

One would be hard pressed to take sides here; it is a genuine Hobson's choice; MAD deters by promising the unthinkable at the cost of an alliance—there is no credible way to extend MAD. Counterforce admits of extended deterrence—but at the cost of pursuing much more usable nuclear weapons programs and systems.

Dellums's style of thinking illustrates how tricky any logic connecting strategic thinking with weapons can be. As an advocate of MAD, and a foe of counterforce or its newer formulations, such as countervailing force or "viable warfighting defense,"[13] Dellums's dislike of the navy's Trident programs is understandable. "Further, the Trident II missile is a first-strike/counterforce weapon. Its numbers and accuracy will destabilize the strategic balance. If its accuracy cannot be accomplished, given problems with reentering the atmosphere and communication disruptions from satellites, it is also unnecessary and wasteful."[14] On the other hand, Dellums is no kinder to weapons with a more second-strike or retaliatory profile.

> Our military planners are still captivated by the idea of a manned bomber. They are not able to see that in the age of ICBM and submarine launched ballistic missiles, the manned bomber has no place in delivering nuclear weapons. In the event of the nuclear war it would get there after the exchange is over and life on earth has ended. This massive machine is out of date. It is designed for high altitude flying but must fly low to evade Soviet radar. Soviet air defense will preclude any penetration by the early 1980s and with the plane not ready for deployment until late 1986, it would provide only four years operational capacity at the most. As a cruise missile carrier it is too expensive and more sophisticated than is needed.[15]

Dellums is clearly an obdurate critic of the Pentagon and the weapons budget; he does not approve of counterforce weapons because of their war-fighting implications; he does not like new countervalue weapons on the grounds that they would be superfluous after all the counterforce weapons he opposes had been exploded in a nuclear exchange.

This is paradoxical, but our purpose here is not to resolve paradox but to illustrate some points about defense critics. We have seen economic critiques. Dellums supplies us with critiques drawn from strategic thinking—even though it is conventional and dated.

The rationale behind Dellums's approach to defense thinking lies in his view of the contemporary world. In his words, "the 'unrest' in the contemporary world has not been 'caused' by Soviet power but by conditions of injustice and human degradation. What must be recognized is the Soviet government's ability to act as a political scavenger among the Third World's neocolonial remains."[16] We turn now to something more futuristic.

The last two points that President Reagan mentioned in his strategic package were enhanced command and control structures and a closer look at strategic defense. These concerns are conceptually quite distinct. Command, control, communications and intelligence—C^3I—are vital operational aspects of any strategy. But they are not a strategy. Strategic defense, on the other hand, can be thought of as a strategy—or at least as a major element in a strategy.

The basic idea behind U.S. strategic iterations (massive retaliation, mutual assured destruction, flexible response, counterforce, countervailing force, and viable war fighting) has been an assumption that these forms of deterrence are made necessary by the impossibility of defending against nuclear delivery systems—especially ballistic missiles and cruise missiles.

On the other hand, C^3I and strategic defense have both moved technologically away from the vacuum tube and the family bomb shelter toward highly imaginative use of satellites. C^3I and strategic defense are also inextricably linked in a logical tangle. Good C^3I bolsters (makes plausible) war-fighting nuclear technologies; it makes for good counterforce. Good strategic defense promises to make counterforce weapons obsolete.

This is not an unalloyed benefit. People may not like MAD or its descendants. But they have the virtue of fitting under the conceptual umbrella of deterrence. Strategic defense is outside of this tradition. But, as we have mentioned indirectly, there is an anomaly in that both deterrent and defensive strategies are technically dependent on satellites. In the early winter of 1983, Senator Mark Hatfield (R, Oregon) said:

> Military space systems, particularly surveillance and warning satellites and command and control systems, have played a critical role in preserving the peace for the last two decades. The military surveillance systems of the United States and the Soviet Union have contributed immeasurably to peace by reducing the elements of surprise to a potential attacker and thereby, the perceived advantage of a first strike. Space systems provide time for analysis, confirmation, consultation, and deliberation,

and reduce the potential for hair trigger responses to ambiguous situations. They have also provided the technical means of verification which have made arms control possible.[17]

As Hatfield continued his speech, he made a number of points about the direction weapons planners were taking:

> Antisatellite weapons (ASATs) now threaten to negate the beneficial and stabilizing influence of surveillance and warning satellites....
>
> As long as there are nuclear weapons and delivery systems for them, the United States and the Soviet Union are going to need space surveillance systems to provide some measure of stability....
>
> Allowing the arms race to extend into space will greatly increase the danger of nuclear war by putting at risk our satellite warning system, creating a situation where accidental war is highly likely, and compounding the destabilizing fear caused by new nuclear weapons with first-strike capability....
>
> We must act now, before an arms race in space adds yet another uncontrollable dimension to the nuclear arms race.[18]

Hatfield's comments were followed by those of Senator Paul Tsongas (D, Massachusetts). He echoed much of what Hatfield argued and then added, "Already underway is the next, still more costly, step in the space war: Weapons to destroy ballistic missiles, including Star Wars-style laser and particle beam weapons. Such systems are not just science fiction; they are now being developed, both in this country and in the Soviet Union, for deployment before the end of the century."[19] Tsongas ended his speech to the Senate by introducing a resolution calling on the president to begin bilateral talks with the Soviet Union seeking a treaty prohibiting ASATs or orbiting weapons (Senate Joint Resolution 28).

This survey of congressional reactions to the Reagan package of strategic proposals has concentrated on foes of his general approach. Given the fair measure of success Reagan has had with Congress, it is obvious that there are also a great many defenders of his views.

STRATEGIC WEAPONS:
THE CONTINUING DEBATE OVER THE MX

It is hard to argue with the proposition that no single weapons system has generated more controversy in Congress than the advanced U.S. ICBM project, the MX missile. Debate over the issue has spanned four presidencies. In the Senate alone, recent full-dress debates were held in December 1982 and in May, July, and November 1983. They are unlikely to be the last. President Reagan hoped to quell debate through the appointment of a bipartisan President's Commission on Strategic Forces—also known as the Scowcroft Commission.

The Scowcroft Commission issued its 29-page report in April 1983. In testimony before the Senate Foreign Relations Committee the following May, Scowcroft made a number of observations about the concerns of his Commission's report. He first noted "that every proposal for arms control and modernization of our strategic forces over about the past decade has become embroiled in increasingly partisan debate, increasingly divisive debate." He continued by pointing out that the United States was looking, in its modernization program, for land-based missiles, for improved survivability, accuracy, command and control, and low operating costs.[20]

The MX fits into this program in three ways, continued Scowcroft. He argued that the MX demonstrated national will and cohesion, that it would rectify an assymetry with Soviet forces in that the MX would pose a counterthreat to those posed by Soviet systems capable of hitting hardened targets, and that it would induce the Soviet Union to negotiate in the direction of stability. Scowcroft went on to place MX deployment in the context of long-range U.S. desires for deploying a smaller, single-warhead missile, and to base future arms talks on counting warheads rather than launchers or missiles.[21]

Scowcroft's report and testimony summarize much of the argument in favor of the missile; curiously, many of the same arguments are turned against the same missile. What kind of missile is it? Why has this still undeployed piece of esoteric technology become a household word while hundreds of similar Soviet missiles carrying thousands of warheads remain largely unknown and unmentioned? We can preface a discussion of the MX by noting a fairly well-known fact about the destructive potential of weapons in general: destruction is enhanced more by accuracy than by yield. In general, it is more effective to work toward hitting the target closely. The lesson is that it is often more fruitful to work on guidance technology than on yield technology. This is especially the case in the instance of missiles designed to hit hardened targets such as an adversary's missile silos. Soft targets, such as cities, can be struck effectively with less accurate weapons. In the case of the MX, it appears that U.S. weapons designers have worked on both accuracy and yield to come up with a very deadly system in blueprint.

The MX fits into a generic class of ICBMs that were first deployed by the Soviet Union between 1974 and 1979. The three Soviet models are known in the West as the SS-17, SS-18, and SS-19. The SS-17 holds four 750-kt reentry vehicles (RVs), the SS-18 holds ten 500-kt RVs, and the SS-19 holds six 550-kt RVs. By way of comparison, the MX is designed to hold eleven 335-kt RVs (MK12a) and, eventually, twelve 500-kt advanced ballistic reentry vehicles (ABRVs).

None of this is particularly remarkable by itself. In terms of yield, the MX is broadly comparable to Soviet systems. But the engineering specifications for the MX call for accuracies in the range of one-tenth to one-twentieth of a nautical mile—around 300 feet. Deployed Soviet systems are estimated to be not quite so accurate; the most precise system, the SS-18, has an accuracy of about 0.14 nautical miles—one third the accuracy of the MX fitted with ABRV.

This combination of accuracy and yield can be calculated by fairly simple formulas to give indicators of destructiveness known as lethality, single-shot-kill-probability (SSKP), or countermilitary potential. The SSKP of a missile is essentially a measure of its theoretical technical capacity for employment as a counterforce weapon; the measure takes into account countermilitary potential and the hardness of the target. The measure is an expression of how likely a single warhead would be to destroy a silo and any missile held in it. Using this standard, the MX is the most powerful weapon on the horizon. With an off-the-shelf Mk12A RV (335 kt), the MX has an SSKP of 0.76; armed with a follow-on warhead, the SSKP will rise to 0.99. Soviet weapons fare rather badly by comparison, with SSKPs ranging from 0.35 to 0.62 (for the SS-18). The MX is also, unlike all three Soviet rockets, solid fueled. This makes it very quick to launch.[22]

Whether or not the technical characteristics of the MX square with its strategic and political goals is what most of the MX debate is all about. It is not a trivial intellectual problem to organize one's thinking about an issue as complex as the MX; it is even harder to organize the thinking of Congress. One of the common concerns, however, about the MX lies in its military role, its lethality is designed around the concept of counterforce. That is, it is not designed to hit cities in a second-strike retaliatory fashion as are older U.S. thermonuclear weapons delivered from any leg of the triad. Instead, the MX has (or will have, if deployed) an ability to strike heavily protected Soviet weapons or launch sites. In this sense, the MX transcends notions of mutual assured destruction (city trading) and opens up possibilities for what is called damage limitation targeting. Essentially, the MX goes beyond deterrence and is a war-fighting weapon. It is also a kind of defensive weapon in that it is analogous to traditional artillery concepts of counter-battery fire.

The MX has drawn criticism from several senators, including Joseph Biden (D, Delaware), Gary Hart (D, Colorado), Patrick Leahy (D, Vermont) and Daniel Moynihan (D, New York). All four voted against financing the development and eventual deployment. A few quotations from an article by Senator Moynihan show the basic reasons of those who voted against the MX. Fundamentally, the argument is destabilization of the balance of terror or undermining the deterrence principle upon which the United States had been basing its security for nearly three decades. Moreover, Senator Moynihan also raises the question of survivability.

> In April of this year [1983], after reviewing 34 basing modes and examining the state of the American deterrent force, the President's highly regarded Commission on Strategic Forces recommended that we deploy the new MX missile in *the very Minuteman silos whose vulnerability had caused us to look for a new basing mode in the first place*. Reagan passed this extraordinary recommendation to the Congress with his endorsement, and this week the Senate will complete its consideration of the legislation that will authorize that the scheme be put in place.
>
> For the first time, the U.S. will have deployed a nuclear weapon in a fashion we *know*—and *they* know—cannot survive a first strike. (Already there are at least two Soviet warheads dedicated, as they say, to each Minuteman silo.)
>
> The MX is so powerful and so accurate, in fact, that it possesses "counterforce" capability—that is, the ability to destroy a heavily fortified, or hardened, Soviet missile silo. A counterforce weapon, deployed in sufficient numbers, can undermine deterrence regardless of how it is based. It can, if known to be powerful and accurate enough, raise the possibility that it will be used to conduct an effective first strike, knocking out all Soviet missiles in one blow and eliminating the ability to retaliate.
>
> Thus the MX, a weapon that had the *capacity* to be used to great advantage in a first strike, is going to be deployed in a fashion in which it can *only* be used as a first strike weapon.
>
> "For what purpose have the Americans done this," Soviets will ask themselves, "after 10 years of development and billions of investment?"
>
> They will have no choice but to conclude that the U.S. has abandoned deterrence, and resorted to the long-standing Soviet posture, based on heavy, vulnerable missiles suited to a first strike.[23]

Senator Sam Nunn (D, Georgia), perhaps the best known and most recognized defense expert in Congress, also expressed doubts about the survivability of the MX and its destabilizing nature on the deterrence problem. In December 1981, Nunn issued a statement to this effect on the floor of the Senate that includes the following passages:

There is considerable doubt in my mind about the wisdom of proceeding with an MX program if reasonable survivability cannot be assured. Available data and evidence indicate that hardening (now established by DOD to cost $5.6 billion for 40 missiles for the maximum hardness option) does not provide any additional survivability. This raises serious questions about stability at the strategic nuclear level. It also raises serious questions about expending over $5 billion for "self-deception"—our experts agree that the Soviets today have the combination of yield and accuracy necessary to overcome the levels of hardening contemplated. The MX is not survivable in existing silos, hardened or unhardened. This fact is confirmed by every agency and every expert who has testified including the Air Force, the CIA, the DIA [Defense Intelligence Agency] and knowledgeable outside witnesses. The one exception is the Secretary of Defense, but I have been unable to find a scintilla of evidence or analysis which supports his position. . . .

Since the MX system would threaten their large ICBM force, would the Soviets believe the U.S. has shifted to a launch on attack posture? Would the Soviets then shift to a similar launch on attack posture thus dramatically lowering the nuclear threshold? Would an accidental nuclear war be more likely? Without a survivable MX system, the answers to these questions have been answered in the affirmative by widely recognized experts, including Dr. William Perry, former Undersecretary of Defense.

In a letter to me on October 20, 1980, on the MX system, General Richard Ellis, former SAC Commander, provided the following description about what is destabilizing in the strategic arena: "The most destabilizing strategic situation that can be devised is one in which a major weapon system of a superpower could be destroyed in a surprise attack by another superpower. To use such a vulnerable system before it was destroyed might then become an attractive military option. For this reason, the Soviets could consider a vulnerable Minuteman force as a first-strike 'use it or lose it' system since it could not survive an all-out attack. MX, on the other hand, will be able to ride out a Soviet attack; therefore, it is both a less tempting and a less threatening element in the U.S. force." Mr. President, if a vulnerable Minuteman is destabilizing, a vulnerable MX would be even more so.[24]

Later (1983) Nunn coauthored with Senator William Cohen (R, Maine) the so-called build-down proposal of nuclear forces, which has its intellectual source in the vulnerability and destabilizing character of the MX and which we will discuss in detail in chapter 5.

Whether indeed the MX can be used as a first-strike weapon simply because it has counterforce capability may be doubtful. Counterforce capability, while necessary for a first strike, may not be sufficient for a first strike. The numbers of weapons, in superfluity, have to be there.

The Reagan administration does not seem to envisage deployment of the MX in sufficient numbers to threaten enough Soviet silos for a first strike; 1,000 warheads, even MX warheads, do not seem to be enough. Impressive numbers of Soviet missiles would be unaffected by an initial MX attack. Yet, as plans progress to deploy a naval analogue to the MX, a submarine-launched counterforce missile called the D-5 or Trident II, in the mid-1990s, the United States will be acquiring quite a threatening counterforce and first-strike potential. There is sometimes a feeling that in the 1990s the United States will reverse the "window of vulnerability" or "window of coercion" opened by the SS-17, SS-18, and SS-19.

At present, these systems potentially threaten the land-based leg of the U.S. deterrent force (that is, the Minuteman missile). Thus, as we have seen, a major congressional concern is to what extent U.S. interests are served by trumping the USSR in a game that has changed, not just quantitatively but also qualitatively, the arms race. By qualitatively we mean that counterforce weapons, unlike countercity weapons, tempt the other side into a preemptive strike against other counterforce weapons. Currently, counterforce weapons are all land-based—their locations are known. Thus, they have a problem with vulnerability. They are also tempting targets.

Most Soviet systems, it appears from SSKP estimates, could destroy very ruggedly protected U.S. silos with three warheads. Since a missile like the MX can carry up to 11 warheads, the economies of attack (3 get you 11) are very tempting. One Soviet system alone, the SS-18, has the lethality and the numbers (over 3,000 RVS) to hit each U.S. silo with three 500-kt warheads. This would leave the United States, some "window of vulnerability" theorists suggest, with nothing but soft-target retaliatory weapons; should they be launched the Soviets would still have enough untouched missiles in stock to attack most U.S. cities. Would a U.S. president assure the destruction of U.S. cities to avenge 1,000 missiles in remote areas of the nation? In the eyes of some, a president would be tempted to compromise or capitulate on the grounds that the United States could hit no Soviet military targets; it could only engage in a fruitless exchange of cities. Thus, what we are pointing out is the argument that in a counterforce situation there is an advantage to the attacker—provided it is certain that the weapons will work on the first strike.

The essential problem with large numbers of counterforce weapons is that they clearly pose a threat to nuclear stability. Representative Albert Gore, Jr. (D, Tennessee) has been one of Congress's most articulate spokesmen on the topic of stability. He captured much of the nature of the stability problem inherent in counterforce systems in the summer of 1982 when he remarked on the floor of the House that "in some future moment of crisis, the last thing we should want is for decision makers on either side to be under a compulsion to launch a nuclear war, for reasons that have to do with the mechanical characteristics of the weapons themselves. On the contrary, we need to make sure, if possible, that weapons in being—in the qualities and in their relationship to each other—do not add to the uncertainties and fears that threaten to drive events out of control in periods of great tension."[25] In Gore's view, one of the dangers in the U.S. negotiation stance, at least in the administration's early proposals for the Strategic Arms Reduction Talks (START), lay in creating "nuclear arsenals which, though smaller, would be both deadlier and mutually vulnerable."[26] What he had in mind was the fact that reducing the numbers of launchers (Reagan proposed a 5,000-warhead limit on 850 missiles) would increase the ratio of warheads to launchers; were the warheads engineered to counterforce lethality there would be an increased vulnerability on the part of silos and a corresponding increase in the temptation to launch a preemptive strike. Simply put, a high ratio of warheads to targets is destabilizing.

Gore's proposal, presented on March 22, 1982,[27] was to pursue an agreement that would "go to the root of the problem by phasing out land-based MIRVed ballistic missiles, in favor of replacement that would carry only a single warhead." In his speech of August 10, 1983, Gore elaborated on his ideas in reaction to the administration's START proposals, which assumed a 5,000-warhead inventory on both the Soviet and U.S. sides. Gore pointed out that

> the core of this proposal is the common ceiling of 5,000 ballistic missile warheads, which is, of course, the major component of the president's negotiating offer. What I suggest is that this number of warheads should be reallocated in ways which are inherently stable. Specifically, we and the Soviets should phase out—as I have suggested earlier— all our land-based MIRVed ICBMs and retain only that portion of our present ICBM force which is un-MIRVed; our Minuteman II missiles, and their SS-11s. It so happens, moreover, that these missiles exist in nearly equal numbers, 450 to 518, which provides the basis for parity. However, because each country regards these missiles as old, I suggest that they be replaced by a new, lightweight ICBM specifically designed to carry just one warhead. The balance of the 5,000 warheads allotted each side would be deployed at sea, thereby continuing a trend in the evolution of both

sides' nuclear forces which is salutary, because nuclear weapons at sea are likely to remain relatively invulnerable for the foreseeable future.[28]

The overall thrust of Gore's approach was to ensure that there would exist no first-strike capability on either side, that the principle of "essential equivalence" would be maintained, and that an attempt to impose limits on cruise missiles would be undertaken. Moving from principles to hardware, Gore's proposals would drastically restructure the Soviet arsenal. Currently (1984), the Soviets maintain 6,000 warheads on land-based ICBMs, compared to slightly more than 2,000 for the United States. In contrast, the United States deploys about 5,500 warheads in submarines; the Soviet total is about 2,500. Under Gore's proposal, both nations would have 500 land-based warheads and up to 4,500 at sea.

Whether or not this amounts to essential equivalence is arguable on several sides. The U.S. interest in SLBMs is logical not only on technical grounds (quieter submarines and more accurate SLBMs) but on military ones. Until plans for the Trident II (D-5) missile were developed, the United States' SLBM force had strictly a soft-target retaliatory role. It was a classic deterrent force. The Trident II is a counterforce, war-fighting missile—with a first-strike potential, if not capability. As long as the deterrent role is maintained for SLBMs—and technical developments in concealment continue to outpace submarine detection—this kind of force posture will continue to have great appeal to Americans. This does not hold true for the Soviet Union. Aside from the fact that the United States seems to have made Soviet submarines less than invulnerable—or at least less than undetectable—both geography and politics make land-based systems appealing to the Soviets. They have an obvious problem with ports, a long-term Russian imperial problem predating the arrival of communism. Moreover, Soviet military planners have known for some time that land-based missiles are politically important; they are a prestige item in international relations. Land-based missiles are perceived differently from sea-based systems, independently, it appears, of relative military capabilities. There is a final operational question from the Soviet perspective. From all we know in open sources, the Soviet navy still has problems keeping its SLBM force at sea at the rate the U.S. navy does. It is hard to imagine talking them into keeping 90 percent of their warheads on delivery systems that are only semideployed in the Soviet Union's few ports.

The practicalities of Gore's proposal are quite easily questioned, of course. But it has to be pointed out that, in his proposal, he was suggesting a philosophy of stabilization; not seriously pushing a joint order of battle for two superpowers who have different strategic advantages and problems. When the Scowcroft Report was issued in the late spring of 1983, Gore reacted to it in a letter to the president dated May 2, 1983. The letter was signed by Gore and eight other representatives, including two Republicans. No mention was made of the 5,000-warhead limit, or a 500-warhead land-based limit. The letter concerned itself with one topic—the impact of MX deployment on strategic stability. Gore and his co-signers argued that "arms control and force posture decisions should be integrated, and organized around the pursuit of stability. Stability, in turn, requires that neither the United States nor the Soviet Union possess the means to conduct a theoretically advantageous first strike. To achieve this condition requires that both sides reverse the trend toward more highly MIRVed ICBMs and move toward a less threatening force based on single-warhead missiles."[29] The degree of dissent over defense policy in this area is not easy to quantify with any kind of precision. But some of the threat's extent and its qualitative dimensions can be suggested by examining the remarks of various members of Congress. The fact of the matter is that feelings about the MX have changed over the span of four administrations; in no small way have the arguments been conditioned technologically. The two most salient technical aspects of the debate have been centered on the MX's lethality (combination of thermonuclear yield and accuracy) and its basing mode, which substantially affects launch tactics and targeting. Additionally, feelings about the MX have been conditioned by its economic impact. It is expensive as strategic systems go. Finally, objections to the MX—and arguments in favor of it also—are politically based as well. Indeed, it is obvious—and not at all surprising—to find that technical, tactical, strategic, and economic arguments about the MX are fundamentally ammunition in a political struggle.

These major themes emerge over the years; there is no easy way to sort them out. But in November 1983, the Senate debate on the 1984 defense appropriations bill (H.R. 4185) focused much contemporary thinking on MX.

On that day, an amendment to delete procurement funding for the MX came up for debate on the floor at 10:30 A.M.[30] The lead speaker for the deletion amendment was Senator Dale Bumpers (D, Arkansas). His remarks showed more passion than is usually found on the Senate floor; after mourning the futility of speeches, he remarked that "when one feels as strongly about something as I feel about the building of the MX, shared by so many of my colleagues, I feel that it is absolutely essential to make at least one last effort, if for no other reason than to clear my own conscience."[31] Bumpers advanced three principal criticisms of the MX: its cost, vulnerability, and launch tactics.

Cost was one of the most often raised objections. As the debate continued, this issue was raised by Senators Leahy (D, Vermont), Kennedy (D, Massachusetts), Levin (D, Michigan), Hollings (D, South Carolina), Glenn (D, Ohio), Riegle (D, Michigan), and Specter (R, Pennsylvania). Bumpers, in the course of a sharp exchange with Senator Stevens (R, Alaska), argued that the MX cost $17 million per warhead and that this was more than half as much again as the cost of a Trident or B-1 warhead. In an interesting twist to his argument, Bumpers went on to point out, "The Pentagon knows that if the Soviets strike first, only 1 to 2 percent of the missile force will survive in the early 1980s. This means for $17 billion, we get one missile, in a worst-case scenario. That comes out to $1.7 billion per warhead. You can buy a Trident submarine for the cost of one survivable warhead. Not one missile—one warhead. I say that just to point out the absurdity of the cost of this system, completely aside from all of the other very compelling arguments."[32] This theme was echoed to a certain extent by Senator Hollings, who stated, "If you look at those costs and if you are trying to save costs, you should realize that times have changed since we started the MX program and that we can now go two routes: one, with upgraded Minuteman with the exact capabilities as MX in the same silos for $13 billion and thereby save about $17 billion from the $30 billion MX fiasco."[33] What Hollings was referring to was the installation of the MX guidance system on Minutemen and the upgrading of 250 Minutemen with more advanced warheads. This would give the system a hard-target capability by about 1992, compared to MX full deployment planned for 1989.[34]

A second major theme advanced against the MX was the issue of vulnerability. Senator Gary Hart (D, Colorado) recounted during the debate the long-running problems the MX faced in this regard.

> Through 10 years of development and 30 proposed basing plans, survivability has been the raison d'etre of the MX missile project. The Congress rejected each successive basing option because the fundamental requirement of survivability was never met.
>
> Finally, the President appointed the Scowcroft Commission with the express purpose of finding a survivable basing mode for the MX missile. In its decision to advocate basing the MX in existing Minuteman

silos, however, the Scowcroft Commission tacitly acknowledged an increasingly obvious fact: There is no survivable basing mode for a land-based missile like the MX, whose huge size makes only limited mobility possible and whose multiple warheads make an inviting target.[35]

Hart's approach to the problem of vulnerability, however, is muddled somewhat by his reluctance to modernize certain other U.S. forces. He argued that "deploying the MX in vulnerable silos removes any deterrent effect that the MX might have. Because it will be vulnerable to a Soviet first-strike, the MX cannot assure retaliation against the Soviets in order to deter a first strike."[36] Yet, immediately after talking about a Soviet first strike, he commented, "The U.S. presently has enough survivable missiles to inflict unacceptable damage upon the Soviet Union even after sustaining a first strike, a first strike is therefore deterred."[37] This logic can be interpreted to suggest that the technical vulnerability of the MX is compensated for by other retaliatory U.S. systems; if the Soviet Union is, indeed, deterred from launching a first strike, then the vulnerability of the MX is complicated by the existence of other U.S. systems.

What Hart was leading up to was his point that "there are those who still argue that we need to modernize our forces by deploying the MX, but the simple truth is that our means of destruction are already modern enough."[38]

The cost and vulnerability of the MX are certainly the most common arguments against it in the view of its congressional critics. But other troublesome issues were brought up as well. One tactic that might be used to protect the MX in silos at risk to Soviet hard-target capable warheads is called launch-on-warning; a closely related concept is called launch under attack.

The implications of this approach for protecting the MX were explained by Bumpers.

> I tell you what the MX does, Mr. President. It puts us into a launch-on-warning position, which we have never been in. And that is dangerous. We know that the bulk of the Soviet Union forces are land based and ours are not. Out of about 7,500 strategic warheads we have on ICBMs and SLBMs, 5,400 of them are on submarines. That is where we want them because they are invulnerable and, under a START agreement, 70-80 percent of the Soviet strategic forces will be in fixed-base silos, maybe more. What do they think when they see a missile that is a first-strike missile like the MX being deployed?[39]

Senator Leahy followed Bumpers's remarks on this theme by stating, "I am profoundly concerned about what a credible counterforce threat by each side will mean to our ability to retain rational control over the decision to begin a nuclear exchange. Unless the MX and its inevitable Soviet counterpart can be avoided, I am convinced we are on the road to launch on warning on both sides."[40] A U.S. move to this kind of launching tactic (which has been neither confirmed nor denied) would be a change from past policy, which has been one of riding out an attack and retaliating after the nature of the attack has been evaluated. Quick launching tactics put major reliance on electronic systems, including satellites and computers. This approach creates fears of accidental nuclear warfare.

One of the arguments advanced in favor of the MX was its utility in arms talks as a bargaining chip. The Soviet Union is developing its own MX equivalent (that is, a system with superior accuracy to the current counterforce Soviet systems such as the SS-18) called the SS-X-24.

Senator Hart dismissed the idea in the following words:

> Lacking any sound military justification for the MX, the missile's supporters have concentrated on political justifications for the MX.
>
> They argue that the United States needs the MX as a bargaining chip in negotiations with the Soviets, and that we should therefore proceed to deploy it regardless of its destabilizing nature.
>
> The only possible bargaining chip represented by the MX, however, is that we might be tempted to launch a first strike against the Soviets. The threat of mutual annihilation is hardly the kind of bargaining chip that is conducive to arms control. Furthermore, the Reagan administration has repeatedly indicated that it does not intend to bargain away the MX.[41]

Senator Specter also expressed reservations about the bargaining chip approach.

> The administration has argued that progress on the MX provided essential leverage for progress on START. In my view however, our continuation with all other weapons systems and improvements in that strategic modernization program should provide sufficient incentive for the Soviets to bargain seriously in Geneva assuming that they are open to making the deep cuts proposed by the president at all. In that regard, a distinction should be drawn between leverage and a bargaining chip. Since the administration has indicated that even in the face of a successful arms control agreement it did not intend to remove the MX missiles, they cannot correctly be considered a bargaining chip.[42]

CONCLUSION

Congressional thinking about the MX is not Congress at its most sophisticated. There is a good reason for this; the MX is very much the ultimate MIRVed ICBM. It is an old (for the nuclear era) concept as a weapons system and, like its Soviet counterparts on the drawing board, suffers from its first-strike image. Its basing mode contributes to its vulnerability; its number of warheads makes it an attractive target for preemption.

Still, in this debate—and in others on the MX—there were some missing elements. One of the arguments advanced against the MX was its threatening posture against Soviet land-based systems. Senator Bumpers wondered what the Soviets might "think when they see a missile that is a first-strike missile like the MX being deployed?"[43] Indeed, such a missile might be intimidating. But would the D-5 SLBM (which has similar properties) be any less intimidating? Either missile could put the Soviet Union in a launch on warning posture. Counterforce weapons deployed in adequate numbers are essentially destabilizing—even if put on invulnerable submarines—if only because they put an adversary's fixed-site weapons at risk. This is a built-in temptation to launch on warning. There is no doubt that this issue will arise again, in debates regarding the D-5 SLBM and its relationship to the somewhat less intimidating Minuteman, which is only on the drawing board.

There is great awareness in Congress of the problem of nuclear stability posed by the way MIRVed missiles threaten land-based missiles. But at times there is a focus on U.S. systems while threatening Soviet systems are minimized. Senator Leahy correctly pointed out that systems such as the SS-18 are less accurate than the MX; he offered the Senate reassurances that heavy Soviet systems are not as threatening as they might appear. Leahy, as well, suggests that U.S. restraint in deploying the MX might induce the Soviet Union to show reciprocal restraint by not deploying the SS-X-24 in the future.[44] This is an idea not frequently shared; history has been cruel to unilateral restraint on the part of the United States. His colleague Senator Hart expresses a more common set of views. Hart has written against both trusting the Russians and unilateralism.[45]

Where in fact is congressional thinking on nuclear strategy headed? First, there is infrequent optimism about the nature of the Soviet Union as an adversary. Despite the Scowcroft Commission's closing of the window of vulnerability, there is a widespread consensus that Soviet intercontinental systems are intimidating. There is also widespread feeling that the land-based leg of the traditional U.S. deterrent force needs to be rethought—designed away from MIRVed systems that are such tempting targets. Favored approaches include the dispersed and mobile Midgetman, SLBMs, and bomber-launched cruise missiles. This implies an attachment to the longstanding strategy of deterrence—with a desire to achieve it at a lower cost. These ideas are not easily reconcilable with other notions advanced in Congress, such as the "freeze" movement. A freeze might reduce expenditures in the strategic arena, but it hardly squares with the desire to modernize strategic systems in a direction away from vulnerable and destabilizing land-based MIRVs toward less vulnerable and tempting targets. Moreover, the attachment to deterrence can hardly be squared with the Reagan administration's interest in active ICBM defense systems.

NOTES

1. Fred Kaplan, *The Wizards of Armageddon* (New York: Simon & Schuster, 1983), p. 391.
2. Weekly Compilation of Presidential Documents, Vol. 17, No. 40 (October 5, 1981), pp. 1074-1076.
3. Ibid., p. 1075.
4. Ibid., p. 1074.
5. Roger D. Speed, *Strategic Deterrence in 1980s* (Stanford, Calif.: Hoover Institution Press), p. 19.
6. U.S. Congress, House of Representatives, 97th Congress, 1st Session, Department of Defense Appropriation Bill, Report No. 97-333 1982, Report of the Committee on Appropriations, November 16, 1981, p. 307.
7. Ibid., pp. 307-8.
8. Ibid., p. 311.
9. U.S. Congress, House of Representatives, 97th Congress, 2nd Session, Report No. 97-482, Department of Defense Authorization Act, 1983, Report of the Committee on Armed Services (April 13, 1982), p. 219.
10. U.S. Congress, House of Representatives, 97th Congress, 1st Session, Rept. 97-71, Part 1, Department of Defense Authorization Act, 1982, Report. p. 186.
11. Report No. 97-482, p. 215.
12. Ibid., p. 214.
13. Caspar W. Weinberger, Secretary of Defense, Annual Report to the Congress, Fiscal Year 1984, p. 34.
14. Report 97-482, p. 216.
15. Ibid., p. 215.
16. Ronald V. Dellums, with R. H. Miller, H. Lee Halterman, and Patrick O'Heffernan, *Defense Sense: The Search for a Rational Military Policy*, (Cambridge, Mass.: Ballinger, 1983), p. xxvii.

17. *Congressional Record*, Senate Vol. 129, No. 9, February 3, 1983, p. S1081.

18. Ibid., p. S1081.

19. Ibid., p. S1082.

20. U.S. Congress, Senate, 98th Congress, 1st Session, Committee on Foreign Relations, Hearings on the President's Commission on Strategic Forces, p. 2.

21. Ibid., p. 3.

22. *Congressional Record*, Senate, Vol. 129, No. 151, November 7, 1983, p. S15530.

23. Daniel Patrick Moynihan, "Reagan MX Plan Commits U.S. to 1st Strike Policy," *Newsday*, July 26, 1983.

24. Statement by Senator Sam Nunn on the floor of the Senate, December 2, 1981, mimeograph provided by Senator Nunn's office.

25. *Congressional Record*, House, Vol. 128, No. 108, August 10, 1982.

26. Ibid., p. H5606.

27. *Congressional Record*, House, Vol. 128, No. 29, March 22, 1982, pp. H994-H1001.

28. *Congressional Record*, House, Vol. 128, No. 108, p. H5607.

29. Letter addressed to President Reagan from Representatives Albert Gore, Jr., Norman D. Dicks, Les Aspin, Vic Fazio, Thomas S. Soley, Richard A. Gephardt, Dan Glickman, Joel Pritchard, and George O'Brien, May 2, 1983.

30. The sponsors were Senators Bumpers, Leahy, Hatfield, Hollings, Riegle, Hart, Sasser, Kennedy, Cranston, Levin, Ford, Proxmire, Tsongas, Bradley, Sarbanes, and Glenn.

31. *Congressional Record*, Senate, Vol. 129, No. 151, November 7, 1983, p. S15544.

32. Ibid., p. S15548.

33. Ibid.

34. Congressional Budget Office, *Modernizing U.S. Strategic Forces: The Administration's Program and Alternatives* (May 1983), p. 9.

35. *Congressional Record*, Senate, Vol. 129, No. 151, November 7, 1983, p. S15555.

36. Ibid., p. S15555.

37. Ibid., p. S15555.

38. Ibid., p. S15555.

39. Ibid., p. S15522.

40. Ibid., p. S15524.

41. Ibid., p. S15556.
42. Ibid., p. S15559.
43. Ibid., p. S15522.
44. Ibid., p. S15524.
45. Gary Hart, *A New Democracy* (New York: William Morrow, 1983), p. 162.

4
WARFARE IN THE EUROPEAN THEATER: DIVIDED OPINIONS IN CONGRESS

NATO ENTERS THE MID-80S

The United States, just like any other nation, possesses permanent interests rather than permanent allies. Nonetheless, of all the defense commitments made by the United States, none is more taken for granted than the ties of alliance with the NATO nations. NATO's conventional land forces are an impressive collection of personnel and arms. The assorted NATO military units are made up of 2.6 million troops divided into 84 divisions. NATO deploys 13,000 main battle tanks, 8,100 guided weapon launchers, almost 11,000 large guns (above 100 mm; of which 1,000 can fire nuclear rounds), 30,000 armored personnel carriers and infantry fighting vehicles, 400 attack helicopters, and 1,800 transport helicopters. NATO's air arms include almost 2,000 fighters and ground attack aircraft, of which 800 (F-111s, Vulcans, F-4s, F-104s, Jaguars, and Buccaneers) can deliver nuclear warheads at intermediate range, 740 interceptors, and 285 reconnaisance planes. In the waters surrounding Europe, NATO has an assortment of fleets that include seven carriers, 15 cruisers, 240 destroyers, and 190 submarines, 35 of which are ballistic missile submarines. These forces, and their predecessors, have protected more people longer than any alliance in history. Yet, there are many observers—among them ordinary citizens, for that matter—who fear that NATO will not see its fortieth birthday in 1989. Some fear that before then war will break out between the United States and the Soviet Union, using NATO territory as a convenient battlefield. Others see NATO's internal dissension as an enemy just as implacable as the Warsaw Pact to the east. In the pages that follow, we will summarize the immediate military threat to NATO and then see how leading congressional followers of European affairs view both the Soviet threat and the internal threat to the alliance.

NATO AND THE WARSAW PACT

In the above paragraph we summarized the military potential of NATO. There is no doubt that its array of personnel and equipment forms an impressive military force. NATO's purpose, however, is entirely defensive. Consequently, it needs to be only powerful enough to deter—not powerful enough to threaten or intimidate. To a very great extent, NATO has lived up to its expectations. But its relationship with the Warsaw Pact or Warsaw Treaty Organization (WTO) cannot rest on historical laurels—the relationship is dynamic and in need of constant revision in light of WTO and Soviet capabilities. Thirty-four years of success do not guarantee 35 years of success; much less 40 or more.

Evaluating NATO's future is a complicated process that involves technical, tactical, operational, strategic, and political considerations. NATO is not just a military organization; indeed, it is a classic example of an intergovernmental organization that concerns itself with issues far broader than military planning. Because of this, it is fair to say that, from all aspects of military and political thinking, NATO has been subjected to the gloomiest of criticisms—its success is measured from day to day. The security it provides is constantly challenged by the USSR and by the WTO component members.

The Soviet Challenge

The adversary NATO faces across the borders of several nations is fundamentally different from the kinds of foes Europeans have been used to. Britons, French, West Germans, Italians, and the smaller nations of the West were cultural and economic rivals (and partners) as well as frequent military enemies. In the case of the Soviet Union (but not so many of its satellites), the adversary relationship is strictly military. It is safe to say that Europeans in general regard the USSR as culturally backward; not even the French Communist Party (PCF) regards Soviet politics as a model. Soviet ideas and Soviet money have very little influence in NATO's assorted cultures and populaces. But Soviet arms are very influential.

There are two very good reasons for the influence of Soviet arms. They are of quite servicable quality, that is, lethality; and there are plenty of them—many very close to NATO borders. Starting in 1962, the USSR began to increase its defense spending by about 4 percent a year in real terms until around 1976. From that point on, increases fell to around 2 percent a year, according to CIA estimates revealed by the Joint Economic Committee of Congress in November 1983. This was an enormous effort; during much of this period, the Soviet military was taking proportionately as much out of the economy as the United States military did in 1944—the year of peak military spending for World War II. Years of this kind of investment in research, procurement, and training have created a first-rank military establishment provided with everything from modern assault rifles to the world's most dreaded ICBMs—the heavy, modern SS-18. It probably bears pointing out as well that Soviet equipment is often of much better quality—at least militarily—than is thought. Specialists familiar with Soviet equipment reveal that many Soviet classes of weapons are rough and unsophisticated—but quite rugged and deadly.[1] A rough idea of the quantitative edge the WTO holds over NATO can be gathered from figure 4.1, in which we show comparative numbers of personnel and selected weapons categories. We do not present these data as simple bean counts. The numbers on which figure 4.1 are based on need to be interpreted in light of the differing missions of the two adversary forces. For example, it is certainly arguable that a defensive force like NATO need not match the Warsaw Pact tank for tank. Still, the quantitative imbalance has become so obvious and intimidating that it has assumed a qualitative dimension.

The reason we advance this argument lies in the history of NATO strategy. The quantitative edge of the WTO is not new—just its enormity. In the era of unquestioned U.S. nuclear superiority, the edge was compensated for by a doctrine that called for rapid use of nuclear weapons on the Soviet homeland. Massive retaliation lost its credibility in the 1960s. It became necessary to start thinking of conventional responses to a Soviet attack on NATO. Thus, in 1967, NATO formally adopted a doctrine called flexible responses.[2] This doctrine calls, at least initially, for nonnuclear resistance to an invasion of NATO soil as near as possible to the frontiers separating the two alliances (forward

Figure 4.1. Comparisons of NATO and WTO Forces (WTO forces as % of NATO forces)

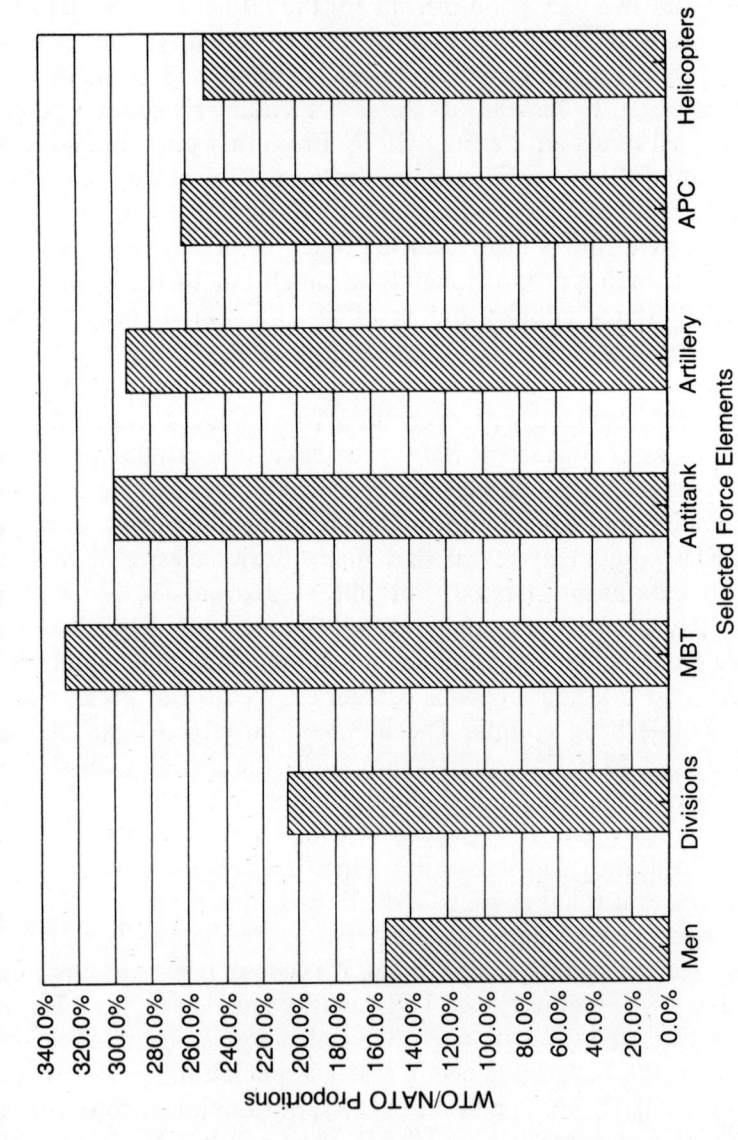

Source: Adapted from *NATO and the Warsaw Pact Force Comparisons*, 1982.

defense). It was understood that should forward defense fail, a nuclear response would be forthcoming. Now, however, both nuclear parity and WTO conventional preponderance threaten this concept.

NATO is in a dilemma in that its great nuclear potential is of limited usability, while its conventional strength is unarguably inadequate. Additionally threatening are changes in Soviet tactics. There are indications that Soviet doctrine is changing to allow much more independent tactics and maneuvering well below frontal or divisional levels. This implies a change from massive frontal assaults—the Soviet style of World War II—toward a true blitzkrieg posture. In other words, just as Soviet nuclear power challenged massive retaliation, Soviet conventional power and its employment currently challenge flexible response and forward deployment.

NATO has responded, to some extent, to shifts in Soviet military posture. A new emphasis has been put on combat readiness. In the past, it was assumed that any WTO attack would be prefaced by very obvious and extended mobilization lead times in the East—lead times that would allow NATO to mobilize. Currently, however, there is a recognition that WTO forces are rather close to being able to attack from a so-called standing start. This is the kind of capability that is particularly menacing to Americans, with their long memory of Pearl Harbor.

Other NATO responses have included the repositioning of ammunition stocks closer to the projected battle zone and the positioning of more troops in northern West Germany. In a sense, NATO has taken some steps toward premobilization. The shift toward the north is a natural recognition of the most likely axis of attack from the east along the flat tank country of northern West Germany. Many U.S. installations are in the southern part of the Federal Republic—areas taken by U.S. troops who were trying to topple Nazis.

NATO has also strengthened command and communications. Battlefield chaos is well known to troops, who accept it as an integral part of combat. It is intolerable to generals. Blitzkrieg warfare and resistance to it require planning and quickly planned responses. The word of where the enemy is, or is going, needs to be passed upward quickly. Orders for the collection of counterattacking forces and their employment need to be passed down quickly. NATO had been notoriously deficient in this area; it is always a problem in polyglot armies formed by democracies. One sign of improvement is the acquisition by NATO of sophisticated equipment such as the airborne warning and control center (AWACS) aircraft.

NATO has learned, as well, from experiences drawn vicariously from wars in other regions. For example, the Arab-Israeli war of 1973 taught numerous lessons that, viewed globally, point to how quickly modern weapons can be destructive of each other. That is, a lot of damage is done by a lot of ammunition in quite a hurry. This implies for NATO a revision of assumptions about the complicated business of logistics. This is not just a matter of where ammunition stockpiles are; it includes planning for rates of consumption and attrition of both matériel and men. Both have to be replaced.

Another NATO response to the WTO buildup has been more attention to what still appears to be an intractable problem: interoperability. In WTO armed services, all equipment is Soviet—or at least Soviet designed. WTO armies use the same weapons that fire the same caliber bullets. Their planes use the same missiles and draw on the same stock of parts. Aside from details of tailoring, one WTO platoon, regiment, division, or army is rather like any other. Equipment and weapons can be freely substituted. NATO's situation has been scandalously different. There is a genuine problem of standardization. It is easy to understand in a genuine alliance as contrasted with an empire that conscripts its satellites. The struggle for weapons that work together, that have standard components, has been uphill in NATO. National concepts of tactics and operations differ. This leads to certain preferences in weapons. Just as importantly, various NATO parliaments are reluctant to spend their defense allocations on interoperable weapons purchased abroad if there is a chance domestic employment can be bolstered, even at the expense of interoperability. NATO may never solve the problem completely. But, just as the WTO has a weakness in the unreliability of satellite troops (Poles, Czechoslovaks, Hungarians, etc.), NATO has to worry about the problems posed to successful operations by its pluralistic approach to weapons and munitions.

The Internal Challenge

Thus far, we have concentrated on NATO's material inadequacies in the face of the Warsaw Pact. These inadequacies are impossible to explain in economic terms. The combined economies of the NATO nations are double the size of the combined WTO economies. NATO's population is 50 percent larger than that of the USSR and its European satellites. Yet, the Soviet Union and the Warsaw Pact have full nuclear parity with clear advantages in intermediate land-based nuclear forces (SS-20) and they have marked conventional superiority.

This is accounted for by political rather than economic problems. The problems lie on both sides of the Atlantic. From the U.S. perspective, it has to be noted that the long-term outlook of U.S. political culture is isolationism in international affairs. Isolationism may be impossible in practice, but this does not mean that U.S. administrations (and public opinion) do not pine for it. U.S. involvement in global affairs was late and reluctant. It is still grudging and is becoming increasingly so toward Europe. Georgia's Senator Sam Nunn noted the extent of U.S. disillusion with NATO when he reported to the Senate Armed Services Committee, "Some have suggested that we simply pull U.S. troops out of Europe in order to punish our NATO allies. As satisfying as this might be as a vehicle for expressing American frustration, it is a recipe for the destruction of NATO and for a neutralized Western Europe."[3] Nunn himself is certainly (obviously from the above) no isolationist. What kind of "American frustration" is he talking about—a kind of frustration that might lead to an abandonment of Europe "to punish our NATO allies"?

Nunn's Republican colleague from Maine, William Cohen, stated the matter in a dramatic speech delivered to the German American Roundtable on March 15, 1982. "It has to do with perceptions," he said of American frustrations, "—about Afghanistan, Poland, the Persian Gulf, and ultimately about the nature of the threats and the nature of the adversary that we face. There is the deep seated and widespread perception in America that we are making a greater military commitment to the defense of Western Europe than Europe is willing to make for itself."[4] Cohen acknowledged a variety of European grievances against the United States, including reduced military spending on the U.S. side in the 1970s, the lack of a U.S. draft, U.S. aid cutoffs to Turkey, the fact that it was the United States that prevented détente, and U.S. reluctance to acquire West European armaments products. Still, he argued that "the growing hostility in America has to do with the perceptions that while we still may share the same ideals and interests that have served to unite us, that there is a fundamental disagreement over the social and military trends that threaten to undermine their very existence." In other words, many European criticisms of the United States simply missed the real point. Americans, thus, have reacted with frustration and hostility.

Cohen was brutally frank to his audience about the split between the United States and Europe over events in Afghanistan and Poland. Europeans, he said, "saw Soviet action as borne from necessity, as defensive aggression." As for Poland, he charged that in Europe, "it was said to be an internal matter for the Poles to resolve and surely not a matter for the alliance to react to with sanctions."

But, if Cohen scored Europeans for failure to follow the U.S. lead, he also had an eye to certain U.S. policies in which, he said, "we trip over our premise and sprawl all over our conclusions." Among them, our failure to push the Polish government into default for its foreign debt, to cancel an International Harvester deal with the USSR, to cancel the Helsinki accords, and to restrict research exchanges with Soviet scientists.

He then chose to take a look at a problem he clearly felt most strongly about, the Yamal Pipeline for delivering gas from Siberia to Europe. Cohen wondered aloud if it were the responsibility of the United States to "deploy a $20 or 30 billion Rapid Deployment Force to the Middle East while Europe helps to build a natural gas pipeline from the Soviet Union?" He argued that "we cannot defend the Persian Gulf without the assistance of our friends and we will not defend it alone, not unless we reduce our commitments in Europe.... There is absolutely no justification for NATO's reluctance to either help defend other areas of vital interest or compensate the United States for undertaking the task. Moreover, common sense as well as military logic would dictate that we stress and expand our force projection capabilities while others provide for the defense of their homelands." Cohen clearly felt strongly about the issue of the pipeline and the Rapid Deployment Force. He said, "And, if I may paint a more graphic picture of the intensity of my feelings on this issue, I believe that Europe is walking toward the Berlin Wall with its eyes closed and may one day find itself behind it with its hands up." These are strong, almost harsh words. But Cohen had a theory to explain what he saw as unacceptable European and, for that matter, U.S. policies. "We, as you, love profits more than we hate communism and totalitarianism." He saw a basis for a renewed Atlantic understanding, even if it were to be based on recognition of a mutual vice rather than upon admiration of a mutual virtue. He made suggestions for a burden-sharing pact premised on the following notions—notions that are controversial and yet innovative.

First, Cohen came out strongly against economic cooperation and technology transfers with the East. He opined that "what we have succeeded in doing to date is to stabilize and strengthen communist societies without reducing their brutality or oppressiveness."

Secondly, he argued that "the U.S. is no longer in a position to defend Europe's forward defense and at the same time meet the new strategic demands confronting it in Third World areas."

Third, he argued that a major expansion of U.S. force levels would not be forthcoming because of both political and economic factors.

Fourth, the United States was going to have to devote more effort to sea power and power projection capabilities outside of the NATO area.

Fifth, the above points would "require a reduction in active U.S. ground forces in Europe so that they can be reconfigured and redeployed to other more vulnerable and volatile areas of the world."

Sixth, Europeans would have to take up more of the burden in defending themselves against an attack from the East.

Senator Cohen's expression of his views was outspoken, even cruel. But they still do not display an attitude that could be called Europhobic. By this term we mean attitudes that are compatible with notions of punishing Europe as a result of personal as contrasted with political motives. Nonetheless, Europhobia exists in some forms and is found in Congress. Senator Larry Pressler (R, South Dakota) comes closest to expressing an archetypal Europhobia. In the late fall of 1983, as the Senate was debating final passage of the 1984 defense appropriations, Senator Pressler addressed the Senate on his views regarding the status of U.S. forces in Europe. He opened his remarks with the following observations:

> Some time ago I took the time to visit our troops in Germany. I was very impressed with their dedication and commitment. I was also troubled at some things I observed, namely the high cost to U.S. taxpayers of maintaining these troops. I was told stories of how the local population does not accept American troops in Germany very well, stories of how the United States is charged high fees for road repairs and bridge repairs when we have a convoy on maneuvers. In general I was told we are not really so welcome in Germany in spite of all our efforts. In fact, we are being taken advantage of by paying the price of defending Europe while the Europeans spend a fair amount of time criticizing us without making an equal contribution.[5]

Pressler went on to introduce an amendment to the 1984 defense appropriations bill calling for a 50 percent reduction of U.S. military personnel over a five-year period. In explaining his amendment he referred to a Senate predecessor, Mike Mansfield (D, Montana) who had made repeated analogous efforts during the 1960s. Pressler went on to query the Senate: "Must our troops be stationed in Germany forever? I hear stories from South Dakota soldiers—and I met with several when I was over there—about how the local population does not welcome them. Our soldiers are subject to double-standard treatment and hostile attitudes, especially when they are in uniform, and there is a strong strain of anti-Americanism. Yet, at the same time, our taxpayers are paying the bills."[6] Pressler received considerable sympathy in the debate from John Stennis (D, Mississippi) and Ted Stevens (R, Alaska)—but the latter two persuaded Pressler to withdraw his amendment, subject to an agreement that the issue would get further study; Pressler himself noted, "I agree that, with the deployment of the Pershing missiles, it perhaps would be the wrong signal at the moment to pass an amendment that would provide for a 50 percent reduction over a 5-year period."[7]

The issue of the extent to which U.S. "taxpayers are paying the bills" is troublesome to NATO members. The conventional imbalance, alone, argues for greater NATO effort. In 1982 NATO nations spent $297.5 billion dollars for defense. This exceeded WTO expenditures substantially. Senator Nunn noted, however, the disparity between expenditures and consequent military capabilities. "The North Atlantic democracies possess more than half again as many people as the Warsaw Pact countries and more than twice the gross national product of the Warsaw Pact countries. In spite of these advantages, the loosely organized NATO defense efforts produce a collection of forces that are quantitatively inferior, qualitatively uneven, and have only a limited ability to rearm, repair, reinforce, support, supply, or even communicate with one another."[8] Part of this problem is financial. In 1978 the NATO nations agreed to a long-term defense program, which committed the alliance to a series of 3 percent real increases in defense spending. U.S. spending under Reagan has exceeded this goal, while European spending has lagged. This has created some transatlantic bickering. Senator Joseph Biden captured the spirit of the debate when he wrote that spending effort comparisons are a matter of perspective. The Europeans tend to look at the entire decade of the 1970s, when U.S. spending declined by 15 percent while European spending went up over the same period by 17 percent. But it is a continuing irritant to Americans, as Biden pointed out, that the United States "provides over 55 percent of NATO military spending while enjoying only 45 percent of the aggregate gross domestic product (GDP). This American contribution is made through an allocation to defense of more than 5 percent of GDP, as compared to an average of 3.4 percent among the other allies. Since such a discrepancy can no longer be justified by facile reference to American prosperity— the United States now stands only seventh in the alliance in per capita GDP—burden sharing will inevitably remain an issue."[9]

Another aspect of the NATO disarray lies in perceptions of the scope of the alliance. Often the leaders of NATO nations wish to avoid commitments to the United States beyond the Tropic of Cancer; NATO's traditional boundary. But increasing European (and Japanese) dependence on Persian Gulf oil, coupled with a supply-interdiction-oriented Soviet navy, has inevitably drawn attention to the link between NATO and the Southwest Asia region. Biden noted this connection as early as 1981. Senator Hart, as well, sees a need to widen NATO horizons. He has expressed concern over the growth of the Soviet navy and the threat its numerous attack submarines pose to Western lines of trade and communication.

Senator Jack Garn (R, Utah) also thought troop limitations would be an appropriate message to Europeans who were "aiding and abetting the enemy"; and Republican Senator John Rhodes (R, Arizona) believed that Europe had ceased to count and that the U.S. commitment to European defense was out of date.[10]

On the other hand, Senator Nunn wants an increase in effective fighting strength in Europe, which may well require more, rather than less, U.S. manpower. He urged a rethinking of Europe's forward defense in a statement on March 13, 1983.

> A large gap exists in NATO's ability to implement the sacred principle of forward defense. NATO is thus confronted with a choice: either to drop the concept of forward defense as part of NATO's doctrine; or to convert forward defense from a theory into a reality by reallocating the NATO defense burden.
>
> U.S. ground forces are and must remain a vital part of the defense of Europe. To properly implement the new Army-Air Force doctrine of "Airland Battle,"[11] our forces must emphasize maneuverability and flexibility, lighter reinforcements, special operations forces, communications, and second echelon attack.
>
> The Allies, however, must increasingly provide the basic ingredients for Europe's initial forward defense, including heavy ground forces, more effective utilization of their vast pool of trained reserves and the possible employment of barrier defenses. In short, if U.S. forces in Europe are to assume the primary responsibility for disrupting and destroying Soviet second echelon forces, European units must assume the primary responsibility for holding the first echelon in check.
>
> In my judgment, the United States should take steps over time, in close consultation with our allies, to make these shifts. If the Europeans do not adjust, military gaps which presently exist will quickly become even more pronounced.
>
> If it is politically essential that forward defense remain a key part of NATO's strategy, it is no less politically essential that our European

allies explain to their citizens why they are not providing the forces to implement the forward defense of their territory.[12]

In terms of strategy for the conduct of a war in Europe, Nunn expressed the view that Eastern Europe would not be a sanctuary if the Soviets invaded Western Europe and that Eastern Europe might well be a political Achilles' heel for Moscow. He added:

> It should be made clear to the Soviets that, in the event of European war, violence will not be confined to Western Europe—that their forces in or passing through Eastern Europe will be subjected to attacks ranging from deep aerial strikes to commando and partisan raids.
>
> To wage war against NATO, the Soviets must move massive forces and supplies from Western Russia across Eastern Europe including Poland and Czechoslovakia, countries whose peoples have long resented—and occasionally resisted—membership in the Soviet empire. In a war we should not permit Moscow to count upon their continued, even if enforced, loyalty. In the 1950s, we trained and fielded special stay-behind forces dedicated to disrupting Soviet military activity in occupied territory and to promoting indigenous popular resistance. This concept should be revived; the very recreation of such forces would strengthen deterrence by putting the Soviet Union on notice that it could not expect a free ride in Eastern Europe in the event of an invasion of Western Europe.[13]

While Senator Nunn attempted to reshape military strategy in Europe, perhaps including a reorganization of NATO's conventional forces, Senator Ted Stevens (R, Alaska), Senate majority whip and chairman of the defense subcommittee of the Senate appropriations committee, did not want to discuss, in the fall of 1983, any changes in U.S. troop strength in Europe. Following the West European wave of agitation against the deployment of Pershing II and cruise missiles, which generated U.S. resentment because it was thought to be action in response to West European desires, Senator Stevens considered it prudent to await more definite reactions to the modernization of U.S. theater nuclear forces.[14]

Despite the concern and perhaps unhappiness expressed by influential senators about tendencies toward neutralism and pacifism displayed by substantial numbers of West Europeans and the difficulty of persuading the European NATO allies to assume their fair share of the financial burden for the common defense (a view shared in 1982 by 68 percent of U.S. respondents questioned by a Harris Poll[15]) the Europeans have a few friends in Congress. One of them is Democratic

Senator Joseph R. Biden, Jr. (D, Delaware), who repeatedly has expressed sympathy on the floor of the Senate and elsewhere for European views. Biden believed that some of the West European reservations about fully supporting NATO's goals were the result of confusion created by the Reagan administration. In November 1981, he explained his thoughts as follows:

> Arriving in office, the Reagan administration boldly promised a foreign policy characterized by competence and coherence. But as yet it has supplied little of either, relying instead on a confused but belligerent rhetoric that has accomplished nothing other than to exacerbate the problem of confidence among America's allies....
>
> The issue of coherence reaches to the military realm as well. In his decision on MX missile deployment, the President obviously took serious account of citizen opposition to certain proposed basing modes. Yet on what grounds, the allies have wondered, has the Reagan administration treated so gingerly with public concern in the United States but so disdainfully with comparable discontent about new missile depolyments among a West European populace which already lives amidst the densest concentration of nuclear weapons in the world?
>
> Put another way, how do we explain that we are not going to base a missile system we say is essential to our security out in the southwestern desert of the United States of America because of citizen opposition and then, somehow fail to understand that there is some reason why the Europeans would be a little upset about the placement of weapons in their area of the world? It is a little like placing the MX system in New York City or placing it in Washington, D.C. or placing it on the east coast.
>
> In sum, since the administration is demonstrably capable of accommodating its anti-Soviet doctrine to political and economic considerations here in America, by what standard can we chastise our allies for contemplating the same? Can we really expect our NATO partners to rally to a policy which has been not only unpersuasively simplistic in theory, but also has appeared hypocritically incoherent in practice?[16]

The sympathetic understanding reflected by Senator Biden, however, has not carried the day. Rather, U.S. government displeasure with European foot-dragging as expressed by Senator Cohen and other senators has prompted warnings to the West European allies that they must assume greater responsibility for their own defense or face cuts in U.S. military support. But growing U.S. impatience with the Europeans may sow further alienation and encourage the kind of neutralist sentiment that Washington and especially the West German government wants to prevent. This impatience may also have motivated a remark by U.S. Undersecretary of State for Political Affairs Lawrence S. Eagleburger at a seminar that U.S. interests might dictate a turn toward the Pacific and away from Europe. This remark created apprehension among top West German leaders, who were later told by Vice President George Bush that Eagleburger's comments had been misinterpreted.[17]

Perhaps complementing Senator Nunn's call for the European allies to provide the necessary forces for an effective forward defense of Western Europe, Henry Kissinger suggested, in an essay in *Time*, radical reforms of NATO.[18] They included the appointment of a European as NATO's supreme commander, allowing the European allies to take control of negotiations with the Soviet Union on nuclear and conventional weapons based in Europe, and withdrawing up to half of the 320,000 U.S. troops if the allies refused to increase their military effort. Kissinger's ideas aroused debate and dissension. One high West German foreign ministry official described them as "irrational pessimism."[19] Although Kissinger's plan is designed to counter neutralist and pacifist trends in Europe, NATO officials warned that it may have the opposite effect, a prediction with which we tend to agree and a concern also expressed by Senator Nunn as early as 1982.[20] There is suspicion that Kissinger may have ambitions to succeed George Shultz as U.S. secretary of state, and, if this is the case, this ambition may well have been the motivation for this latest plan.[21] We may remember Kissinger's widely heralded "Year of Europe," announced in April 1973 in the Netherlands. It was to serve the revitalization of the European union idea, but it also carefully distinguished between the "global" interests of the United States and merely the "regional" interests of Western Europe. It was a misguided effort on the part of Kissinger, and the latest plan may not fare much better.

On the other hand, the concept of a more vigorous use of conventional weapons in the defense of Western Europe, which is inherent in the Nunn concepts presented earlier, may find acceptance by West European leaders. Clearly, a strategy of quick use of nuclear weapons is becoming increasingly unpalatable in the West and, therefore, perhaps less credible in the eyes of Soviet military leaders. Hence, conventional defenses need to be bolstered by NATO so that it could resist a Soviet attack for weeks and successfully counterattack without resorting to nuclear retaliation. Advanced electronic systems can give new speed and precision to conventional weapons and thereby enhance their combat power. Obviously, this would involve additional cost and higher taxes for Europeans, a cost that at least for nuclear deterrence has been so far borne by U.S. taxpayers. But many problems will have to be solved before a shift in strategy as outlined above and indicated by Nunn could be realized. France would have to agree that French troops would be permitted to reinforce NATO front lines rapidly, and the West Germans would have to accept the fact that the new strategy would make a battlefield of both West and East Germany. Indeed, the mere adoption of this strategy by the government of the Federal Republic might harm the improving ties between the two Germanies, a high-priority goal of Bonn. Of course, regardless of what strategy were to be followed, an attack by WTO forces would create havoc in the two Germanies.[22]

Regardless of what motivated Kissinger to articulate his proposals, NATO is at a critical juncture financially and strategically. A recent DOD chart (figure 4.2) shows that the United States and its NATO allies spend more for defense than the Soviet Union and its WTO allies. Yet, the WTO is credited with substantially more conventional military capability than NATO. Some of the answers to this puzzle lie in the WTO's comparatively low military manpower costs; but, as Senator Nunn points out, a large part of the combat imbalance lies in the WTO's greater degree of force integration and commonality in weaponry and tactics. Nunn continues:

> The present NATO armaments system functions as little more than a loosely organized collection of national defense efforts, backed by fragmented and highly inefficient national procurement systems. The North Atlantic democracies possess more than half again as many people as the Warsaw Pact countries and more than twice the gross national product of the Warsaw Pact countries. In spite of these advantages, the loosely organized NATO defense efforts produce a collection of forces that are quantitatively inferior, qualitatively uneven, and have only a limited ability to rearm, repair, reinforce, support, supply, or even communicate with one another. No less disturbing are the wide disparities in national ammunition stockpiles which call into question NATO's ability to sustain combat beyond the first weeks of hostilities.... Integration and interoperability can produce quantum jumps in military effectiveness, but this type cooperation continues to elude NATO leadership. National military traditions and inter-service customs have for years sapped NATO's resources and strength.[23]

Nunn, as noted earlier, proposed a new conventional strategy for NATO that is based on the "air-land battle" doctrine under which NATO forces attempt to isolate the attacking first echelon of WTO

Figure 4.2. Comparison of NATO and WTO Total Defense Costs

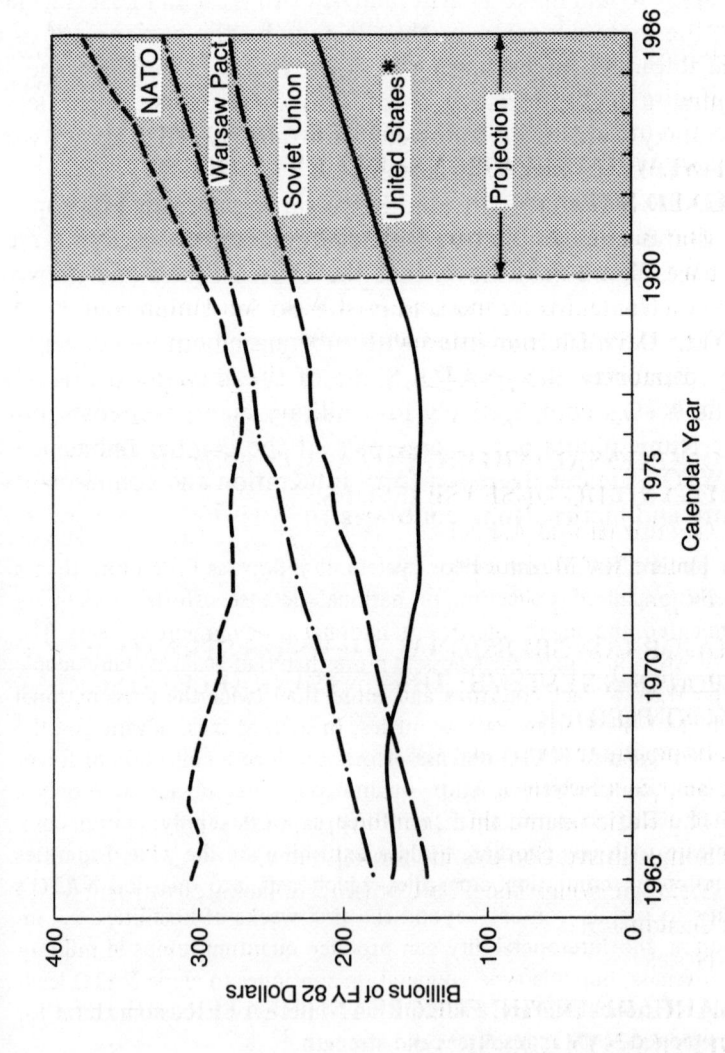

*Southeast Asia Increment Excluded.
Source: Department of Defense Posture Statement FY 1982.

invaders from reinforcing echelons—through attacks on the latter—and thereby destroy the momentum of the invasion. In addition, integration and interoperability of weapons must be given highest priority. Nunn opposes any "no first use" of nuclear weapons policy as it would denude the effectiveness of any NATO defense,[24] a position with which we fully agree. If NATO were willing, however, to dedicate itself to creating a new, credible conventional defense, putting conventional deterrence on a much firmer basis than that at present, then serious consideration could be given to a policy of "no first use" of nuclear weapons.[25]

NOTES

1. A high-ranking Russian officer who defected to the West recently wrote, "I hate the Communists, but I love Soviet weapons. The fact is that Soviet designers realized, decades ago, the simple truth that only uncomplicated and reliable equipment can be successful in war." Viktor Suvorov, *Inside the Soviet Army* (New York: Macmillan, 1982), p. 182.

2. An early description of flexible response comes from former Secretary of Defense MacNamara. "What we are proposing is a capability to strike back after absorbing the first blow. This means we have to build and maintain a second strike force. Such a force should have sufficient flexibility to: (1) strike back decisively at the entire Soviet target system simultaneously; or (2) strike back first at the Soviet bomber bases, missile sites, and other military installations associated with their long-range nuclear forces to reduce the power of any follow-on attack—and then if necessary, strike back at the Soviet urban and industrial complex in a controlled and deliberate way." Secretary of Defense, Annual Report FY 1964, p. 28.

3. U.S. Congress, Senate, Congress, Session, Committee on Armed Services, *NATO: Can the Alliance be Saved?* Report of Senator Sam Nunn to the committee, May 13, 1982.

4. Cohen's remarks are taken from the transcript of a speech delivered to the German American Roundtable, March 15, 1982. The text was provided by Sen. Cohen's office. Subsequent quoted excerpts are taken from the same source.

5. *Congressional Record*, Senate, Vol. 129, No. 150, November 4, 1983, pp. S15437-38.

6. *Congressional Record*, Senate, Vol. 129, No. 151, p. S15438.

7. Ibid.

8. Senator Sam Nunn, *NATO: Can the Alliance be Saved?*, p. 9.

9. Joseph R. Biden, Jr., "Leading the Allies," *Washington Quarterly* (Summer 1981), reprint, p. 4.

10. *Economist*, January 7, 1984, pp. 21-23.

11. According to U.S. Army experts, the essence of this new military doctrine is a more effective and innovative utilization of existing forces and new technologies to exploit vulnerabilities in Soviet doctrine and force structure. This proposed army doctrine would give emphasis to the attack of all Warsaw Pact echelons. For the first time, this doctrine points to the need to attack the follow-on, reinforcing echelons of the WTO forces before they cross the inter-German border and to seize the initiative early through defensive counterattacks against them on NATO territory.

12. Sen. Sam Nunn, statement of March 13, 1983, pp. 8-9.

13. Ibid., pp. 5-6.

14. *Economist*, January 7, 1984, p. 21.

15. Ibid.

16. *Congressional Record*, Senate, Vol. 127, No. 170, November 19, 1981, p. S 13682.

17. *International Herald Tribune*, March 1, 1984.

18. *Time*, March 5, 1984.

19. *International Herald Tribune*, March 1, 1984.

20. Senator San Nunn, *NATO: Can the Alliance be Saved?*, p. 7.

21. *Neue Zuercher Zeitung*, March 6, 1984.

22. *International Herald Tribune*, February 28, 1984.

23. Senator Sam Nunn, *NATO: Can the Alliance be Saved?*, pp. 17-18.

24. Ibid., p. 20.

25. For Nunn's detailed recommendations, see ibid., pp. 22-27.

5
NUCLEAR WEAPONS FREEZE AND ARMS CONTROL

FREEZE AND PEACE MOVEMENTS

In the United States, a movement to freeze nuclear weapons by Washington and Moscow became a political phenomenon in the early 1980s. Americans, who had not experienced the ravages of war in their country during the twentieth century, suddenly became aware of the enormous destruction of lives and property that would be wrought by a nuclear exchange. Up to that time, most Americans believed that the medical profession and hospitals would be able to provide necessary care and restoration for victims of a nuclear holocaust. An organization called Physicians for Social Responsibility, headed by a Boston pediatrician, Helen Caldicott, tried to disabuse them of this notion. Doctors would not be able to save people if nuclear war came. Millions would die at once, and few, if any, physicians would be left to treat the millions wounded (mostly burned) and those disabled by radiation.

A book by Jonathan Schell entitled *The Fate of the World*[1] added to the concern and fear of many Americans. It described in vivid detail what nuclear war would mean and argued that preventing the destruction of humanity was a moral imperative superseding all other values. The impact of the book was enormous and materially strengthened the freeze idea, originally conceived by Randall Forsberg, an arms control specialist. This idea had led to a large number of teach-ins on U.S. campuses and town meetings in many states where the freeze, the MX missile, NATO problems, and related issues were discussed. On June 12, 1982, 750,000 people marched in Central Park in New York City in the largest political demonstration in U.S. history.[2] Many organizations, for example, the League of Women Voters, expressed their support for the freeze movement, and during the elections in November 1982, ten states passed resolutions in favor of a bilateral freeze of existing nuclear arsenals.[3] A number of freeze supporters were elected to Congress, whose House of Representatives passed a watered-down version of a mutual, bilateral, verifiable freeze resolution in 1983 by a narrow margin. However, such a resolution failed in the Senate, and the Reagan administration opposed the concept as damaging to U.S. interests.

In Western Europe, the peace movement has a much longer history. During the Korean War, millions signed a Stockholm Peace Resolution, an action stimulated at least in part by the Soviet Union. In Great Britain, the Campaign for Nuclear Disarmament (CND) has been active for many years, but television "newsworthy" demonstrations did not occur until the so-called double-trade decision by NATO was announced in December 1979, according to which the Pershing II and cruise missiles were to be installed by the end of 1983 unless a satisfactory agreement between the United States and the Soviet Union led to the dismantlement of the Soviet SS-20 missiles.

It was the 1981 decision by the Reagan administration to reverse a Carter decision and to build the neutron bomb or Enhanced Radiation Weapon [ERW][4] that set off the largest set of propeace demonstrations Europe had ever seen. In October 1982, 200,000 marched in Bonn; and, in November of that year, 400,000 marched in Amsterdam. Huge marches took place also in Paris, Rome, Madrid, and Barcelona. Demonstrations of equal size were organized again in the fall of 1983, especially in West Germany and Great Britain, to halt the deployment of U.S. Intermediate Range Nuclear Forces (INF) weapons, but the protests failed. In December of that year, Pershing IIs were installed in West Germany and cruise missiles in Britain.

The sources of the European peace movements have been varied. The Catholic and Protestant churches have contributed to their strength and have given the movements a moral tone. The ecologists such as the "Greens" in West Germany had a considerable input and through such political organizations as the party of the Greens have injected a strong political flavor. Left-wing political orientations have also been infused by leftist supporters of the Social Democratic Party in the Federal Republic and similar tendencies of socialist parties elsewhere. Finally, various Communist Party stands have been apparent, and it is quite obvious that the Soviet Union has attempted to exploit the peace movements to its own advantage and to promote its own objectives.

CONGRESSIONAL OPPOSITION TO THE NUCLEAR FREEZE

Although there has been a strong grassroots movement for a mutual and verifiable freeze of nuclear weapons by both the United States and the Soviet Union and an appropriate freeze resolution, though watered down, was passed by the House of Representatives in 1983, albeit by a small margin, it is noteworthy that even some of the representatives and senators who voted for the freeze did so with some misgivings. Obviously, it is easy for the Soviet Union to urge a nuclear freeze since the count of land-based strategic and long-range theater nuclear weapons is favorable for its side. But, in spite of the understandable anxiety of most Americans to see the danger of nuclear war reduced, to negotiate a nuclear freeze is far from easy and, in fact, much more complex than it appears at first glance. This can be seen best from some very thoughtful comments made by Representative Albert Gore, Jr. (D, Tennessee), who voted for the freeze, and by Senator Patrick Leahy (D, Vermont) who is a supporter of the freeze but who in a statement on the floor of the Senate gave a full picture of the complexities of this approach to peace. We will also quote a strong opponent of the freeze, Representative Henry J. Hyde (R, Illinois), who provides interesting arguments in support of his position.

Gore, who is rapidly gaining a reputation as one of the foremost experts on defense policy, warned in an editorial in the *Washington Post*:

> Congressional advocates of a freeze will face an especially painful dilemma. A pattern of votes against nuclear weapons programs adds up to unrequited concessions to the Soviet Union. But a pattern of votes in favor of such weapons adds up to approval of a process that will rapidly erode the freeze as a viable policy for a future administration. . . .
>
> The freeze resolution which I have supported states an ideal we are not going to see realized, even pursued, by the present administration. Meanwhile, Congress—and the country—need some basis for a discrim-

inating and, in the end, cathartic debate over our course of action. Given the right outcome, we might find areas of agreement strong enough to put consensus, rather than controversy, behind the president in dealings with the Soviet Union.[5]

Senator Patrick Leahy, in whose state of Vermont in 1983 7,000 high school students from 30 schools had debated the nuclear weapons freeze and nearly 73 percent of them had worked in favor of such a measure, also had some cautious words to say on the floor of the Senate. He stated that, in order to be successful, a well-defined proposal for a freeze must be articulated that would provide a realistic basis for genuine negotiations with the Soviet Union. So far, there is insufficient analysis of the form a verifiable freeze-based proposal would take, making it vulnerable to legitimate concerns and questions raised by sceptics. He added, "The controversial nature of the freeze initiative has meant that what has been done so far is primarily advocacy by supporters or criticisms by opponents. It has been, for the most part, a monolog of the committed. The debate cries out for finding of fact and objective statement of issues. Both sides want meaningful, verifiable arms control which enhances national security and stability. They differ on how to get there."[6] A sample of a convinced opponent's arguments in the House of Representatives debate on the freeze demonstrates the accuracy of Senator Leahy's statement. Representative Henry J. Hyde, knowledgeable on defense matters and a persuasive speaker, opposed the freeze resolution with the following remarks:

> Now, I look at this resolution and frankly I am bewildered. What is it? It is incoherent. Let us look at a few of the phrases here. "Whereas the greatest challenge facing the Earth is to prevent the occurrence of nuclear war by accident or design." Well, I would have hoped the imagination of the draftsman might have included "within the framework of freedom and justice and dignity." I would say the greatest challenge is not just to prevent the occurrence of nuclear war, we can do that today, just disarm, just lay down our arms and get on our knees and face east. But to do it within a framework of freedom and justice, to do it within the framework of our oath of office which requires us to uphold the constitution, which says, in addition to "provide for the common defense," it also admonishes us to "secure the blessings of liberty for ours and for our posterity."
>
> So, I gently impeach the language of the very first sentence in this "Resolution."[7]

Mr. Hyde condemns the resolution on the basis of the hierarchy of values implicit in the document with which he disagrees, and later in his speech he points out that 75 percent of the U.S. nuclear weapons are on launchers 15 years and older, whereas the same percentage of Soviet weapons is on launchers 5 years and younger, and that 70 percent of the Soviet weapons but only 25 percent of the U.S. weapons are ICBMs. However, he failed to address the much more crucial problem of identifying precisely the nature of the nuclear weapons freeze desired. Senator Leahy understood this problem and asked the Congressional Research Service (CRS) to analyze a comprehensive force approach as well as other possible alternatives based on the freeze concept. He said on the floor of the Senate:

> I was aware that the study would raise issues that freeze proponents, like myself, would find difficulty in resolving. But because I am in earnest about seeking a viable alternative to the present arms control stalemate, I accepted this challenge. A far greater challenge exists today with the two key arms negotiations deadlocked, and with both sides moving ahead with new weapons which may make verifiable nuclear arms control all but impossible in the near future.
>
> ...this is not a study tailored to support either side in the controversy. I suggested no premise, asking merely that CRS concentrate on the critical issues which arise in a comprehensive freeze as well as other, narrower freeze approaches. I did not expect definitive answers. CRS does not have sufficient resources or analytical capabilities to undertake more than a preliminary review. Nevertheless, I hoped it would identify in one document both the potential arms control advantages and the issues necessary to consider in structuring a freeze proposal.[8]

CRS FREEZE APPROACHES

The CRS study distinguishes four approaches to the formulation and negotiation of a freeze on nuclear weapons. Each has different military and political implications.[9]

Proposal 1 is a *comprehensive freeze* under which the United States and the Soviet Union agree to a freeze on the production, testing, and deployment of nuclear weapons and their delivery systems.
Implications:

> This proposal bars the testing, production, and deployment of systems not currently deployed.
>
> It includes both strategic and intermediate/theater systems, as the only defining term is *nuclear weapons*, regardless of range or size.
>
> Depending on the definition of *deployment*, it could bar the replacement of current weapons with weapons now in storage. Implicitly, both force structures will therefore be frozen in place and subject to deterioration over time. This could decrease reliability as well, given the ban on testing, if maintenance efforts alone prove to be inadequate.

Proposal 2 is a *first strike weapons freeze* and envisages a freeze by both superpowers on the production, testing, and deployment of all ballistic missiles, including warheads and launchers, regardless of range.

Implications:

> Like Proposal 1, it bars the production and testing of systems not yet deployed.
>
> It still covers both strategic and theater systems, but only those involving ballistic missiles.
>
> The issues of deterioration and reliability remain relevant.
>
> Opportunities would exist and be attractive for rechanneling arms efforts into those areas not frozen.

Proposal 3 envisages a *strategic weapons freeze* covering the production, testing, and deployment of all strategic weapons, including warheads and delivery systems.

Implications:

> This proposal uncouples strategic and theater forces.
>
> It continues to freeze the destabilizing first-strike strategic systems.
>
> SALT definitions of what constitutes strategic systems could be used to define included and excluded systems.

Proposal 4 aims at a *freeze of force levels* as established in the SALT II Treaty and at the other treaty terms as well (i.e., limits on certain new systems, sublimits on specific types of systems, but probably without the allowance for one new light ICBM).

Implications:

> Like Proposal 3, it uncouples strategic and INF issues.
>
> It continues to freeze the destabilizing first-strike strategic systems.
>
> It would make formal the SALT II agreement, which both the United States and the Soviet Union have tacitly agreed not to undercut.

More limited freezes than those outlined in the four proposals are also conceivable. For example, the most dangerous ICBMs are those that can be launched cold and that are easily reloadable, and therefore a freeze could be limited to these vehicles. Another limited freeze could apply to ABMs, whose extensive and sophisticated development could be highly destabilizing. Finally a freeze could be confined to cruise missiles, which, however, poses a severe problem of monitoring. Indeed, monitoring the freeze raises serious problems with respect to all four major proposals. Cooperative measures between the Soviet Union and the United States would be required for all proposals, most for Proposal 1 and less for the other three. There is no doubt that the monitoring and verification issue poses major problems, which can have strong military and political effects. In this respect, it is useful to quote the CRS study, which has been made part of the *Congressional Record* by Senator Leahy.

> There is a distinction between the military and political demands for monitoring. While U.S. officials would like to have as much information as possible on Soviet arms activities, it is generally assumed that there will be gaps. How significant these gaps will be is one of the factors that goes into assessing the confidence in monitoring any provision. Another is the likelihood that any gap could result in a significant military gain by the Soviet Union. However, more rigorous standards must be applied to monitoring when considering the maintenance of public support for current and future arms control agreements. Indications, or even serious suspicions about Soviet non-compliance will undercut domestic support for arms control among the public at large and within Congress. Congress experiences a particular problem, as it has not always received all of the information it felt it needed on the resolution of compliance issues.[10]

Although freeze proponents have attempted to make the public believe that the nuclear freeze concept could be made available immediately, negotiations over as complex an issue as a freeze would most likely be as lengthy as those for SALT, START, or INF. The reason is not only the complexity of monitoring and verification but also the difficulty of fully understanding what a particular set of freeze conditions would mean for the military establishments of both countries since the institution of a freeze affects credible deterrence, crisis stability, and systems deterioration. The Soviet Union may now call enthusiastically for a freeze, but, regardless of the propaganda value of such a call, the Kremlin would still be intent on working out the details since it would want to retain the perceived advantages of U.S. nondeployment of the MX and the D-5 Trident missiles as the result of a freeze while reducing the susceptibility to new vulnerabilities in its arsenal.

The effect of a freeze on NATO also needs to be explored carefully. While each proposal would appeal to the general European desire for arms control and for a reduction of East-West tensions, it would also raise the question of NATO's ability to respond to Soviet INF improvements already in place (especially Proposal 1), and each proposal would heighten concerns about the credibility of the U.S.

Table 5.1. Comparison of Major Freeze Proposals

Proposal	U.S. Domestic Reaction Positive	U.S. Domestic Reaction Negative	Allied Reaction Positive	Allied Reaction Negative
Proposal 1: Freeze on the production, testing, and deployment of all nuclear weapons and their delivery systems.	1) Public support for a freeze.	1) Reaction of those who feel U.S. is vulnerable. 2) Limited economic dividend and increased defense costs in other areas.	1) Desire for arms control	1) Question of credibility.
Proposal 2: Freeze on the production, testing, and deployment of first-strike weapons.	1) Public support for arms control. 2) Addresses destabilizing systems.	1) Disappointment of freeze advocates. 2) Reaction of those who feel U.S. is vulnerable. 3) Limited economic dividend.	1) Desire for arms control. 2) Allows GLCM response to SS-20.	1) Greatest U.S. concern over own territorial security. 2) Question of credibility of U.S. nuclear umbrella.
Proposal 3: Freeze on the production, testing, and deployment of all strategic weapons.	1) Public support for some arms control. 2) Allows NATO GLCM and Pershing II response to SS-20s.	1) Dissappointment of freeze advocates. 2) Reaction of those who feel U.S. is vulnerable. 3) Limited economic dividend.	1) Desire for arms control. 2) Allows NATO GLCM and Pershing II deployment.	1) Continued political problems re NATO INF plans. 2) No INF arms control. 3) Additional pressure for INF agreement. 4) Greater U.S. concern over own territorial security. 5) Question of credibility of U.S. nuclear umbrella.

| *Proposal 4*: Freeze based on SALT II Treaty. | 1) Public support for some arms control. 2) Allows NATO GLCM and Pershing II response to SS-20s. | 1) Disappointment of freeze advocates 2) Substantial opposition to SALT II. 3) Might allow new ICBM development. | 1) Desire for arms control. 2) Allows NATO GLCM and Pershing II deployment. | 1) Continued political problems re NATO INF plans. 2) No INF arms control. 3) Additional pressure for INF agreement. 4) Greater U.S. concern over own territorial security. 5) Question of credibility of U.S. nuclear umbrella. |

Source: Adapted from Table IV, CRS Study of "Nuclear Freeze Alternatives: Monitoring, Military and Political Implications," *Congressional Record*, Senate, May 10, 1983, pp. 3-16.

nuclear umbrella. Only other U.S. defense commitments and expenditures in the conventional arms area would allay allied apprehension.

Finally, it should be understood that a freeze is unlikely to generate large economic benefits. Nuclear weapons are a relatively small part of defense spending. Other defense costs—maintenance of frozen systems to avoid deterioration when reliability can no longer be fully tested and improvements in nonfrozen areas, including conventional forces, to buttress military capabilities—are likely to increase substantially.

For those interested in learning more about the realistic prospects of a mutual and verifiable freeze, reading the full CRS study is instructive. Table 4.1 provides a comparison of the four major freeze proposals including domestic and allied effects and reactions. This analysis clearly indicates that, despite the strong emotional, very understandable, surge for a nuclear freeze, it may not be a sound approach to an early and foolproof prevention of nuclear war so eagerly desired by the American people.

REVIVAL OF SALT II?

The Reagan administration and the Soviet government have agreed tacitly to comply with the provisions of SALT II despite the fact that it was not ratified by the U.S. Senate and in fact expired at the end of 1981. As we have seen in the preceding pages, the CRS proposals for a freeze include one that uses as a basis the terms of the SALT II Treaty. The question then arises why SALT II should not be revived by both superpowers and ratified by the Senate. Indeed, Senator Biden suggested such a revival in 1982. He stated on the floor of the Senate:

> In my own judgment, the appearance in the United States of a substantial arms control constituency is a very positive and long overdue development, one which is likely, in several ways, to strengthen the Atlantic Alliance, on which American security depends.
>
> An immediate effect should be to reassure our allies that Americans and Europeans have not diverged fundamentally on the need to restrain East-West conflict and avoid nuclear war. . . .
>
> Having described these positive aspects of the emergence of a strong arms control constituency, I must draw a distinction between the public movement, from which I draw considerable encouragement, and the specific freeze proposal which I find flawed. One important drawback of a freeze is its impact upon Europe, where the prospect for successful East-West negotiations to limit theater nuclear weapons is heavily

dependent upon NATO's clear and explicit willingness to undertake nuclear modernization if negotiations fail. . . .

From the strategic, as opposed to the theater, perspective the freeze concept is also flawed, and for the very plain reason that we have already negotiated something better and the Soviets have already agreed to it. That agreement is the SALT II treaty now languishing in the Foreign Relations Committee. For American interests, SALT II is far superior to a freeze because it would require the Soviets to begin immediately to dismantle some 250 strategic launchers, which is 10 percent of the Soviet force, now targeted on the United States. It would, moreover, place a verifiable limit—what we call a "fractionation" limit—on the number of warheads the Soviets may place on even their most powerful intercontinental ballistic missiles.

Meanwhile, SALT II would leave the United States unconstrained in implementing the U.S. defense improvements which the Reagan administration has described as a necessary foundation for future arms negotiations.[11]

Senator Biden suggested that it was time for the Senate to vote on and ratify the SALT II agreement, which legally was still alive because President Reagan had not officially withdrawn it. But he also realized that after the many attacks on SALT II during the Carter presidency by many Republicans and conservative Democrats, obtaining the necessary two-thirds majority in the Senate for ratification was not a realistic political option regardless of the immediate benefits that might accrue to the United States. Moreover, the Reagan administration had no interest in reviving SALT II, which it considered severely flawed during Mr. Reagan's campaign for the presidency. Its major objective remains some version of START, which would result in a reduction of strategic nuclear weapons, at the same time bringing about a more favorable balance of ICBMs through the initial deployment of MXs.

THE COHEN-NUNN BUILD-DOWN PROPOSALS

Arms control prospects were given a bipartisan boost in 1983 when Senators Cohen and Nunn announced the mutual guaranteed build-down of nuclear forces. In terms of background, Senator Cohen stated on the floor of the Senate:

While I am sympathetic to the goals of a nuclear freeze, I cannot support it as a policy because it would leave the United States with a vulnerable land-based missile system, a deteriorating bomber force, a submarine fleet that faces block obsolescence in the early 1990s, and no systems comparable to Soviet land-based missiles targeted on Western Europe.

In studying the arguments of proponents and opponents of an immediate freeze, I have noticed that there are a number of essential points of confluence. Both seek to enhance strategic stability through equal reductions in nuclear arsenals. Both agree that any agreement on reductions must be mutually verifiable. Both favor serious, vigorous negotiations with the Soviet Union, aimed at meaningful arms control.[12]

The result of Cohen and Nunn's deliberations was the introduction of Senate Resolution No. 57, which specified that whenever either the United States or the Soviet Union added a new nuclear weapon to its force, two older, less stabilizing weapons must be eliminated. In particular, according to Cohen:

each side would exercise the principle of freedom to mix in determining tradeoffs and force composition.

Useful counting rules and implementation procedures from the SALT agreements could be retained.

The sides would agree on verification measures, including cooperative measures as necessary, which insure confidence in compliance.[13]

According to both Cohen and Nunn, this process would allow force modernization to increase survivability and, thereby, deterrence, while at the same time achieving an actual reduction in overall numbers of weapons. As a consequence, tensions would be reduced, stability of the deterrence system would be enhanced, and the reliability of deployed systems increased. Importantly, these developments would give less cause for turning to strategies calling for hair-trigger responses to perceived threats.

The resolution requested the president to take appropriate action in the context of the relevant negotiations between the two powers and instruct the U.S. arms negotiators to raise the proposal with their Soviet counterparts. Senator Nunn emphasized that:

the Cohen-Nunn proposal for a guaranteed build down concept requires reductions as an integral part of modernization by both the United States and the USSR. Efforts to modernize and reduce simultaneously are compatible, and both contribute to improving stability and deterrence.

One of the strongest arguments in favor of the ongoing modernization is improved survivability of our nuclear systems. Existing, destabilizing vulnerabilities will not be cured by freezing them in place.[14]

The resolution was cosponsored by a number of prominent senators from both sides of the aisle including Senators Hart, Biden, Moynihan, Packwood, and Percy, the chairman of the Senate Foreign Relations Committee.

In a four-page letter addressed to Senator Nunn and dated May 12, 1983, President Reagan acknowledged the merit of the build-down proposal and promised to consider it in connection with the Scowcroft Commission recommendations. But the letter seemed to be mostly oriented toward building bipartisan support for the deployment of the MX ("Peacekeeper" in the President's letter) in order to signal U.S. resolve and thereby persuade the Soviets to agree to a balanced reduction process.[15] Nevertheless, in October 1983, the president instructed the U.S. delegation to call for a guaranteed annual 5 percent mandatory build-down and address concurrently the build-down of bombers and air-launched cruise missiles.

In testimony before the Senate Foreign Relations Committee on June 21, 1983, Senator Nunn enlarged on the build-down proposal. He said:

> The build-down proposal is intended to complement, not supplant, other arms control initiatives. I would expect both the START and INF negotiations to continue while build-down arrangements are being put in place and certainly as it is being implemented. The build-down proposal is intended to bring about rapid and immediate reductions in the two sides' forces while the necessarily more difficult negotiations for qualitative restrictions are taking place.
>
> The build-down concept envisions continued observance of such SALT II provisions as (a) the ban on deployment of new heavy ICBMs, (b) a ban on increasing ICBM and SLBM warhead fractionation beyond those levels specified in SALT II, and (c) the sub-limit on total numbers of MIRVed ballistic missiles.
>
> In other words, the build-down does not repeal the accomplishments of previous arms control agreements. In addition, the build-down does not preclude other types of constraints that the sides might agree to.[16]

As for the question of whether a particular missile such as the Soviet Union's PL-5 is a "new type" or only a permissible variant of the SS-18, such an issue would fall under the definition of *new types* as specified under the SALT II agreement. The U.S. government would have to decide whether to negotiate more precise guidelines or abrogate SALT II if the existing definitions and verification procedures were not viewed satisfactory with respect to PL-5 and other cases.

Further refining the build-down approach, Senators Nunn, Cohen, and Percy suggested a number of principles, which included:

> an immediate ceiling on the number of ballistic missile warheads;
>
> an immediate ceiling on the overall destructive capacity of the strategic forces of both sides at existing levels;
>
> a guaranteed annual build-down in the number of ballistic missile warheads;
>
> the creation of incentives favoring stabilizing systems—in particular, small, single-warhead ICBMs; and
>
> a second guaranteed annual build-down in the overall destructive capacity of the strategic forces, missiles, and bombers of both sides.

The senators also suggested a brief agreement on the elements of build-down prior to the negotiation of a detailed treaty. This would be similar to the Vladivostok Agreement, which President Ford negotiated in 1974.[17]

Addressing arms control in the long term, Nunn had earlier remarked:

> We must recognize that limiting numbers of nuclear weapons under arms control puts a premium on survivable systems if both sides are to begin to move away from a hair trigger.
>
> We must recognize that the United States and the Soviet Union have a mutual stake in preventing nuclear proliferation and in promoting confidence-building measures to guard against war by accident or war by miscalculation.... I would submit that confidence-building measures, such as the joint nuclear risk reduction concept as well as the exchange of visits by high level U.S. and U.S.S.R. military officials I have proposed are perhaps even more important in preventing war over the long run than arms reduction agreements.[18]

Nunn was referring to his suggestions of several confidence-building measures that could have long-range beneficial results for the prevention of a nuclear holocaust. These CBMs would be a joint U.S.-Soviet information-sharing effort combined with a multinational center for crisis management. This center would be staffed with a permanent standing team of highly qualified civilians and military personnel, in full operation 24 hours a day, 365 days a year, with access to the top political and military leadership. This mechanism would give each side more confidence in the facts during a nuclear crisis and might make it easier to determine, independently and jointly, the origin of and parties responsible for any explosion of nuclear weapons. It would encourage cooperation and confidence building between the superpowers, even when political relations are at a low ebb. It could also add a significant degree of deterrence to third-country or terrorist attempts to light a nuclear bonfire.[19]

Although these will not be simple tasks to accomplish, discussions and negotiations should begin even during a period when the Soviets have suspended the START and INF talks. Visits between U.S. and Soviet military leaders have also been proposed by European politicians and retired military officers, who see great advantage from such dialogues. The U.S.-Soviet hot line, which has recently been improved, also plays an important role in the confidence-building process. Finally, some efforts need to be made to lenghten the warning time both countries would have of a nuclear attack by negotiating a possible nuclear weapons deployment agreement.

REALISTIC PROSPECTS FOR THE BUILD-DOWN

As we know, the last arms control agreement negotiated was SALT II in 1979. Although not ratified, it has been adhered to by the two superpowers informally in spite of Reagan's strong attacks on it during his election campaign in 1980.

In May 1982, the Reagan administration offered a new proposal for arms control in the Strategic Arms Reduction Talks. The United States and the Soviet Union, as mentioned in chapter 3, would each cut back its total number of ballistic missile warheads—ICBMs and SLBMs—to 5,000. Of this total, which represented at that time a one-third reduction, neither side would be allowed more than half, or 2,500 warheads, on land-based missiles. Moreover, neither side would be allowed more than 850 ballistic missiles. A second-stage agreement was to put a ceiling on total missile throw weight, to be set below the U.S. total.

The size of the reduction in the U.S. proposal was very large, much greater than the 10 percent suggested by President Carter in the original SALT II proposal. Another new departure was to count mainly warheads rather than launchers, as had been done in the SALT agreements.

The Soviet Union turned down Reagan's specific proposal as unfair, although it did accept the principle of nuclear arms reduction. The reason for the Soviet rejection was the uneven distribution of existing ICBMs and SLBMs, with the Soviets having the majority of their warheads on land-based launchers and possessing a much lower number of SLBMs than the United States. Hence, cutting down the number of land-based ICBM warheads posed little difficulty for the United States, but for the Soviets it would mean they would be left with a much lower total of warheads than the United States.

In addition, the Reagan administration favored the United States in other respects. The limit of 850 missiles happened to be almost exactly half the total that the United States had then deployed. However, the Soviets, with about 2,300 missiles deployed, would have to give up more. When, later, total missile throw weight would be subjected to a ceiling, the Soviets again would have to give up much more than the United States (see table 1.1).[20] Indeed, since the United States has its throw weight "fractionated" across a larger total number of warheads than the Soviet Union, the enormous Soviet throw weight represented fewer warheads because the latter were much bulkier and heavier, and this constituted another disadvantage for Moscow. The Soviet government also complained that cruise missiles and strategic bombers were left uncontrolled in the START proposals, but later, as we have seen, Reagan agreed to their inclusion.

While there has been some forward movement on arms control, and the Reagan administration has indicated its approval of the build-down proposal, it remains uncertain whether the administration is serious about its pursuit. When the original START proposals were made in 1982, there was some suspicion that the Reagan administration's proposals were designed to give the public appearance of being a serious effort at arms control while actually anticipating rejection by the Soviets because of their being very one-sided.[21] In the meantime, U.S. modernization of its nuclear arsenal could continue with the hoped-for deployment of the MX and D-5 missiles and other weapons. Reagan's lack of seriousness in the arms control field also seems to be confirmed by the administration's reluctance to seek a comprehensive ban on antisatellite weapons, as mandated by Congress in an amendment to the fiscal 1984 Defense Department authorization bill, an amendment proposed by Senator Paul E. Tsongas of Massachusetts. According to the administration's spokesman, Larry M. Speakes, the problem is verification, which has been the usual holdup in most arms control endeavors. But, according to Speakes, "the President is certainly willing to talk."[22] Meanwhile, the United States is moving to more advanced systems of antisatellite weapons because the Soviet Union is believed to have such a weapon and the United States needs to have a better one.[23]

With this spirit of weapon escalation so prevalent by both superpowers, it would not be realistic to expect the build-down proposal, although pushed by the greatest military experts and very influential members of Congress, to have much of a chance unless backed by strong and demanding public opinion. In spite of many Americans being aroused about the disaster of a nuclear war, it is doubtful that specific public opinion aimed at such a specialized foreign and defense policy as the build-down would materialize. It is also questionable whether public opinion will be sufficiently strong to be seriously considered by the administration. To a large extent, "The Day After" and the Catholic bishops' pastoral letter have slipped into the background. Of course, the whole question is moot at this writing; the Soviets are not in a negotiating frame of mind.

NOTES

1. Jonathan Schell, *The Fate of the World* (Boston: Houghton Mifflin, 1982).

2. Richard Smoke, *National Security and the Nuclear Dilemma* (Reading, Mass.: Addison-Wesley, 1984), p. 226.

3. Ibid., p. 227.

4. President Carter rejected the assembly of parts produced for ERW. President Reagan decided on the assembly, but stockpiled the weapon in the United States.

5. Albert Gore, Jr., "Cold, Hard Facts on the Freeze," *Washington Post*, December 7, 1982.

6. *Congressional Record*, Senate, Vol. 129, No. 63, May 10, 1983, p. S6360.

7. *Congressional Record*, House, Vol. 129, No. 33, March 16, 1983, p. H1215.

8. *Congressional Record*, Senate, Vol. 129, No. 63, May 10, 1983, p. S6360.

9. The CRS study is reprinted in Ibid., pp. 6361-6369.

10. *Congressional Record*, Ibid., p. S6368.

11. *Congressional Record*, Senate, Vol. 129, No. 9, April 22, 1982, p. S3911.

12. *Congressional Record*, Senate, Vol. 129, No. 9, February 3, 1983, pp. S1109-S1110.

13. Ibid., p. S1110.

14. Ibid., p. S1111.

15. Copy of letter supplied by Senator Nunn.

16. U.S. Congress, Senate, 98th Congress, 1st Session, Committee on Foreign Relations, *Arms Control and the Mutual Guaranteed Build-Down Concept*. Testimony by Senator Sam Nunn, June 21, 1983, p. 4.

17. Letter to General Brent Scowcroft, chairman, President's Commission on Strategic Forces, September 9, 1983.

18. Senator Sam Nunn, *Arms Control*, p. 5.

19. Senator Sam Nunn, "Arms Control: What Should We Do?", *Washington Post*, November 12, 1981.

20. Smoke, *National Security*, pp. 232-33.

21. Ibid., p. 33.

22. *International Herald Tribune*, February 28, 1984.

23. *International Herald Tribune*, February 28, 1984.

6
WHICH ROAD TO PEACE?

Although the peace movements in Western Europe are currently in some disarray and the U.S. nuclear peace movement has declined in political influence, the danger of nuclear war persists. Nuclear strategic and INF weapons are being modernized and continue to be deployed by the United States and the Soviet Union; some of them are potential first-strike weapons. Others such as the MX have survivability problems and are destabilizing. The Soviet Union does not want to return to the negotiating table until, as the new leader Konstantin Chernenko stated in March 1984, "the United States remove[s] the obstacles which it created by fielding its new missiles."[1] This may not be Moscow's last word, but it shows the difficulties in attempting to seek agreement on such arms control proposals as advanced by Senators Nunn and Cohen. Meanwhile, the Reagan administration may, deep in its collective heart, not be unhappy about the Soviet position, although in public it would state otherwise, because it provides opportunities for further nuclear weapons buildups and refinements as well as for engaging in research and development of antiballistic defense and antisatellite measures. As Senator Leahy characterized the situation in remarks at Dartmouth College (New Hampshire) on April 30, 1983:

Arms control is a consuming personal concern, yet never have I felt so discouraged. The future looks increasingly frightening. . . . [T]he dilemma of arms control today is not a lack of ideas. It is a lack of commitment. The arms control process is sliding into a stalemate that could last for years. . . . The main drawbacks are both political and ideological. The unpalatable fact is that leaders in both the United States and the Soviet Union are not serious about subordinating their struggle for power to the overriding need to limit the mortal nuclear danger.[2]

Can the stalemate be overcome? The current circumstances and divergent perceptions of the leaderships of the two superpowers make it unlikely. As Chernenko stressed, the principle of "equal security" for the Soviet Union is paramount, and that means the maintenance of the Soviet advantages in land-based launchers of both strategic and theater weapons. The basic reason for Chernenko's interpretation of security is the Soviet perception of a deep U.S. hostility toward the Soviet Union, which became very clear through the Reagan administration's often expressed conviction that the Soviet Union is the focus of the evil in the modern world, but which also appears to reflect U.S. attitudes during the last two decades, although they were marked by endeavors at détente. Hence, the Soviets may well now doubt the possibility of reconciliation.[3] Indeed, Moscow may now believe sincerely that President Reagan's various derogatory statements about the Soviet Union imply a U.S. desire to dismantle or destroy the USSR. On the other hand, virtually the whole world is declared a zone of vital U.S. interest.

The Russians also seem to believe that some of the Reagan administration's statements about the Soviet Union were insulting and touched deep chords of national pride. They have awakened memories of past interventions by Americans on Soviet soil during the civil war from 1918 to 1920.[4] Of course, Soviet leaders should remember that at the end of World War II the United States was prepared to cooperate with Moscow and that Soviet conduct in Central and Eastern Europe made that impossible and brought on the Cold War. But, whatever the cause of the confrontations that began at the end of World War II, the perceptions of Soviet elites that the United States may seek a denial of the legitimacy of the Soviet state itself may well be political reality, and it is dangerous because it may produce desperate action leading to nuclear war that nobody wants.

Unfortunately, as Moscow is obsessed with fears for its security as a result of Reagan's earlier rhetoric, the Reagan administration is obsessed with international communism. Moreover, high DOD officials such as Richard Perle and Fred Ikle seem to believe sincerely that the West is in a position to break the Soviet Union and should try to do so, although this may not be the expressed policy of the Reagan administration at this time. As William Pfaff states correctly, "it is an important truth that nations should not be pushed against locked doors."[5] Even if the president and his closest advisers see the world locked in a struggle between good and communist evil, and even if he believes that military power is the only guarantor of U.S. safety and the closing of the perceived window of vulnerability, pushing the Soviets too hard may be counterproductive to U.S. security.

Without doubt, Soviet actions such as their brutal behavior in Afghanistan and Poland contributed heavily to the deplorable state of relations between the two superpowers. Moreover, there are troublesome signs that the Soviet Union may be violating some arms control agreements, especially the unratified SALT II, which both sides are informally observing. If indeed real compliance issues exist, they must be solved satisfactorily. But, while they need to be pursued seriously, political posturing should be avoided and no public campaigns should be unleashed against unproven Soviet violations. There is the temptation to use allegations of Soviet cheating to gain support for increased defense spending. In addition, such allegations are likely to lead to claims that the Soviets cannot be trusted to abide by international agreements, an already widely held attitude among Americans; and this could become a cover for a lack of progress in arms negotiations. If indeed Soviet violations are proven, they should be handled through existing channels and appropriate redress sought. If that does not prove feasible, our compliance with SALT II and other arms control agreements should be rescinded, as suggested by Senator Nunn.

On January 16, 1984, President Reagan delivered a speech in which he sent a very conciliatory and clear message to the Soviet leadership and which had an entirely different tone from that of his previous rhetoric. He insisted that while deterrence was essential to preserve peace, it was not the beginning and end of U.S. policy toward the Soviet Union. A dialogue about peace with Moscow was essential to reduce the level of armaments and build a constructive relationship. He said, "We don't refuse to talk when the Soviets call us imperialist aggressors and worse, or because they cling to the fantasy of a Communist triumph over democracy. The fact that neither of us likes the other's system is no reason to refuse to talk. Living in this nuclear age makes it imperative that we do talk."[6] Many Americans, including members of Congress generally critical of Reagan's policies, believed that the president's speech constituted a new departure, but whether the Soviet Union was prepared to accept the administration's offer to return to the negotiating table was far from certain. While it appeared that Moscow was perhaps interested in going beyond SALT II by cutting its missile launchers from 2,250 to 1,800, a reduction of warheads would also be necessary to move toward a build-down. And, despite optimistic forecasts that the Soviet Union would be ready to talk again about the problem of strategic arms reduction, especially since on March 16, 1984, the MBFR talks resumed in Vienna, these negotiations, at least initially, seemed as deadlocked as they had been during the preceding ten years. Indeed, the WTO representative said that he regretted that NATO had returned to the negotiations without making new proposals, and he warned that the decision of the Soviet bloc to return to the talks should not be interpreted as a sign that Moscow had accepted the Pershing II and cruise missile deployment in Western Europe.[7] In fact, the same problems, such as verification and the exact count of WTO troops, bedeviled the discussions, as they had in preceding sessions, although a little progress on the verification issue seems to be in prospect.[8]

The Stockholm Conference on Confidence- and Security-Building Measures, which opened in January 1984, also had made little visible progress and adjourned in March for a seven-week recess. The WTO had suggested the negotiation of a European nonaggression pact, but the NATO nations dismissed such a pact as rhetoric because they claimed that the necessary guarantees for peace existed already in the UN Charter, and discussion of nuclear weapons in any case was outside the mandate of the conference.[9] All this seemed to indicate that the conditions for a movement toward peace were not auspicious, and the impression gained ground among NATO diplomats that it was more unlikely than ever that the Soviet leadership would even consider a resumption of the Geneva talks until after the presidential election in November 1984.[10]

It appears to us that until a better climate can be created between the United States and the Soviet Union, arms control and reduction negotiations will not produce satisfactory results that will assure the prevention of nuclear war. A number of considerations should guide this effort if it is to be taken seriously by Washington.

• The two nuclear superpowers must coexist on this planet. Much as the president may have wished it, the Soviet Union shows no sign of internal collapse, economic or political, in the near future. In fact, 1983 was a very good year for Soviet agriculture.

- The Soviet people are patriotic and are likely to support their government in any crisis. Insulting the Soviet government and system will strengthen the commitment of the Russians to back their leadership even if they are dissatisfied with many aspects of their political and economic system. World War II is the best evidence for this pattern of behavior.
- Although the Soviet government may cheat in their compliances with explicit and tacit agreements from time to time, such violations should be discussed through the channels established for this purpose. Only if clear proof exists that the Soviets will not correct the violation should it be made public.
- The U.S. government should attempt to ratify SALT II despite President Reagan's denunciation of it as "fatally flawed."
- Nuclear one-upmanship should be avoided. A comprehensive nuclear test ban was nearing completion when the Carter administration suspended talks in response to the Soviet occupation of Afghanistan. Testing is not vital to U.S. national security, and some testing can be completed before the ban takes effect. In addition, the pending treaties banning tests above the 150-kt limit for military and civil underground explosions, which both superpowers are committed to respect, should be ratified, and this will put into effect verification procedures including some on-site inspection that has already been agreed upon.
- Negotiations about limiting antisatellite weapons, another casualty of Afghanistan, should be resumed. The security of military reconnaisance, navigation, and communication satellites should be more important to the United States than Soviet defenses. Yet, the Reagan administration has persisted in developing antisatellite weapons that will outperform the more primitive Soviet models that threaten only low-orbit targets. A moratorium on the testing of these weapons would be a first step to halting development and protecting satellites in higher orbits, even if verification problems may delay a total ban.
- Finally, the search for defenses against ballistic missiles should be advanced only with great caution. It would lead to the abrogation of SALT II's limit of ABMs and the agreements banning nuclear weapons and explosions in space. It would completely undermine the deterrence principle, especially when combined with offensive ballistic missiles such as the MX.

If these considerations were to be used for a new approach to the negotiations with the Soviet Union, the prospects for the implementation of the Nunn-Cohen proposals for a build-down of nuclear weapons would most likely be improved. The chances for Senator Nunn's suggestions regarding confidence-building measures discussed earlier, as well as for the gradual institution of periodic meetings between high-ranking U.S. and Soviet officers, may also look brighter. Such meetings would provide opportunities for discussion of divergent perceptions and problems faced by both sides. It is fair to assume that the new approach and suggested actions would receive approval by the

27 senators on both sides of the aisle who cosponsored the intital build-down resolution and would be applauded by many House members as well.

President Reagan, who more recently has shown a remarkable new flexibility in dealing with the Soviet Union (as well as with fiscal matters such as reducing the deficit), could adopt some of the features suggested for a new approach, which may well have the support of many Americans deeply concerned about the horrible consequences of a nuclear war. Indeed, the prevention of such a war, as the president has intimated, has a very high priority in the promotion of the United States' national interests. A beneficial byproduct of this new approach to Moscow would be eager acceptance by most of the NATO allies and the overall strengthening of the alliance's cohesion, which has been badly frayed as the result of recurring frictions. Combining this approach with bolstering NATO's conventional capabilities and adopting new strategies, as proposed by Senator Nunn and other members of Congress, may enhance the security of the United States.

The adoption of an even-handed approach to the negotiations with the Soviet Union of course does not mean espousing everything the Soviets present in the talks. The usual caution must prevail when evaluating Moscow's proposals. But the important thing is a different frame of mind on the part of the administration: less negative prejudice and more of a balanced judgment regarding Soviet motivations. After all, Moscow is just as anxious to avoid millions of casualties as is Washington—in fact, most likely more so in view of the enormous casualties of World War II, which have not been forgotten by the Russian people and must be kept in mind by a leadership anxious to maintain its position of power in the Soviet system.

If, then, the various proposals and suggestions made by some of the foremost military experts in Congress should eventually produce favorable outcomes regarding this most serious issue of war and peace, the curbing of nuclear weapons, the "politics of the unthinkable" may turn out to have had a very salutary effect on mankind.

NOTES

1. *International Herald Tribune*, March 13, 1984.
2. Mimeo, p. 1
3. William Pfaff, "The Kremlin's Message to Americans is Somber," *International Herald Tribune*, March 7, 1984, p. 4.
4. Ibid.
5. William Pfaff, "Moscow Ought to Sidestep This Obsession," *International Herald Tribune*, March 8, 1984, p. 4.

6. *Weekly Compilation of Presidential Documents* (Washington: Office of the Federal Register), Vol. 20, No. 3, p. 43.

7. *The Guardian* (Manchester, England), March 17, 1984.

8. This was the thirty-second round of talks since they began over ten years ago.

9. *International Herald Tribune*, March 17 and 18, 1984.

10. Ibid.

INDEX

A

ABM, 7
ABRV (advanced ballistic re-entry vehicle), 63
active defense, 74
Addabbo, Rep. Joseph, 53, 57
Afghanistan, 31, 83
Airland Battle, 87, 91
ALCM, 7
American Legion, 36
Andropov, Yuri, 24, 25
anti-Americanism (Europe), 85-86
Appropriations, House Committee on, 53
Armed Services, Senate Committee, 42
arms control, 13
ASAT (antisatellite weapons), 61, 110, 113, 117
Aspin, Les, 38
attrition warfare
AWACS (airborne warning and control center aircraft), 81

B

B-1, 6, 27, 32, 38, 39, 43, 50, 53, 70
B-52, 6
Backfire, 12
Badger, 13
ballistic missile defense, 117-118

Barzini, Luigi, 1
basing mode (MX), 69, 89
Belgrade (CSCE), 22
Berlin, West, 20
Biden, Joseph R. Jr., 86, 89, 104
Blinder, 13
bombers, 3, 4, 59, 110
Bradley, fighting vehicle, 43
Brown, Harold, 11
budget, defense, 2
Budget, Defense, 27
build-down, 105-111, 117
Bulganin, 20
Bumpers, Dale, 70, 71-72, 73
burden-sharing, 84
Bush, George, 90

C

C-3 Missile, 50
C31, 50, 58, 60, 81
(command and control), 8, 11
Caldicott, Helen, 95
Cambodia, 46
Canada, 51
carriers, aircraft, 37, 50
Carrington, Lord, 26
Carter, Jimmy, 23, 38, 44, 49, 50, 109
Catholic Bishops' (pastoral letter), 111
Center for Defense Information, 36

Central Committee (Communist Party) of the Soviet Union, 10
cheating, Soviet, 117
chemical weapons, 54
Chernenko, Konstantine, 25, 113
Cheysson, Claude, 16
CIA, 65
civil defense (USSR), 11
CND (Campaign for Nuclear Disarmament), 96
CODA (Congressional Office of Defense Appraisal), 27
Cohen, William, 65, 83, 84-85, 106, 113
Cold War, 19, 114
COMMITTEES, CONGRESS
confidence building measures (CBM), 12, 117
Congress (role in defense), 34-37
Congressional Budget Office, 28
Congressional Research Service (CRS), freeze proposals, 99-104
conscription (draft), 15, 39
conventional defense, 90
costs, weapons, 27-28
counterforce, 58, 63, 66, 73
counterforce, 68, 71
countervalue, 59
crisis destabilization, 54, 57, 58
crisis stability, 51, 58
cruise missiles, 13, 16, 51, 88, 96, 110
CSCE (Conference on Security and Cooperation in Europe), 11, 21-22
Cuba, missile crisis, 46
Cyprus, 44
Czechoslovakia, Soviet invasion of, 21

D

D-5 missile, 50, 68, 73, 101, 110
D-5 missile, 66
deficits, U.S. budget, 27
Dellums, Rep. Ronald, 54, 58
detente, 19-23
deterrence, 8, 58
deterrence, extended, 53, 64
DIA (Defense Intelligence Agency), 65
diad, strategic, 51
draft (conscription, U.S.) *see* conscription (draft)
Dulles, John Foster, 46

E

Eagleburger, Lawrence S., 90
Eden, Anthony, 40
Eisenhower, Dwight David, 19-20, 40
El Salvador, 44
EMT (equivalent megatonnage), 4, 7
enhanced radiation weapons, 16
European Economic Community (EEC), 15
Europhobia (isolationism), 85

F

first strike, 7-8, 61, 64, 68, 71, 72
first use, 15
flexible response, 60
Ford, Gerald, 46
Forsberg, Randall, 96

forward defense, 80, 84
freeze (nuclear), 54, 74, 88, 95-112, 105
freeze, proposals for, 99-111
Garn, Jake, 87
Geneva summit, 20
GLCM (ground launched cruise missile), 13, 25
Glenn, John, 70
Goldwater, Barry, 38
Gore, Albert Jr., 66-67, 68-69, 97-98
grain (Soviet purchases of), 25
Greece, 44

H

Haig, Alexander, 44
Halberstein, David, 40
Harmel, Pierre, 20
Hart, Gary, 70, 71, 72, 73, 87
Hatfield, Mark, 60
Helsinki accords (CSCE), 11, 22, 84
Heritage Foundation, 36
Hiroshima, 4
Hollings, Fritz, 70
Huddleston, Walter, 42
Hyde, Henry, 97, 98

I

ICBMS (intercontinental ballistic missiles), 3
Ikle, Fred, 115
interoperability (weapons), 82, 91, 93
Iran, 46
isolationism (U.S.), 83
Israel, 44

J

Jackson, Henry, 44
Japan, 12
Johnson, Lyndon, 40
Johnston, J. Bennett, 42
Joint Economic Committee, 79

K

Kennan, George, 15
Kennedy, John F., 46
Kennedy, Robert, 46
Kennedy, Ted, 70
Khrushchev, Nikita, 20
Kissinger, Henry, 1, 22-23, 44, 90
Kohl, Helmut, 15
Korea, 40
Korea, South, 12
launch-on-warning, 71, 73
Leahy, Patrick, 70, 71-72, 73, 97, 99, 113
Lebanon, 33-34, 41
lethality, 63
Levin, Carl, 42, 70
logistics
LRTNF (long range theatre nuclear weapons), 13, 82

M

M-1 tank, 42
MAD (mutual assured destruction), 6, 59, 63
Madrid (CSCE), 22
management, military, 26-27
maneuver warfare (Soviet), 80
Mansfield, Mike, 45, 85-86
Marxism-Leninism, 9, 19

massive retaliation, 79
Mayaguez, 36, 46
MBFR (mutual and balanced force reductions), 21, 23, 116
McNamara, Robert, 15, 58-59
Midgetman missile, 62, 73
Minuteman missile, 7, 50-51, 64, 68, 73
MIRVS (multiple independently targeted reentry vehicles), 3, 57, 67, 73, 74
missile crisis, Cuba, 46
Moynihan, Patrick, 64
MX, 6, 32, 43, 51, 53, 57, 61, 63, 64, 65, 69, 70, 73, 89, 96, 101, 110

N

Nagasaki, 4
NATO (North Atlantic Treaty Organization), 12, 13, 14, 15, 21, 79, 96
NATO (military posture), 79
NEACP (National Emergency Airborne Command Post), 8
nerve gas, 16
neutralism (European), 16, 88-89, 90
neutron devices (enhanced radiation warheads), 16
Nixon, Richard, 22, 32, 44
no first use, 93
nonproliferation treaty, 23
Nunn, Sam, 64-65, 83, 86, 87, 88, 89, 91, 105, 106, 108, 113, 118

O

Outer Space Treaty of 1967, 23

P

pacifism (European), 88-89
parity, strategic, 24
peace movement, 14-15
peaceful coexistence, 20
Peaceful Nuclear Explosion Treaty of 1976, 23
Peacekeeper missile (MX), 107
Perle, Richard, 115
Perry, Dr. William, 65
Pershing II, 13, 14, 16, 23, 25, 88, 96, 116
petroleum reserve, naval, 41
Pfaff, William, 115
Physicians for Social Responsibility, 95
pipe-line (natural gas), 25, 84
Poland, 22, 83
Politburo, 10
power projection, 85
Present danger, committee on, 50
Pressler, Larry, 85
procedure (rules in Congress), 40
public opinion (Europe), 16
public opinion (U.S.), 88

Q

quarantine, naval, 46

R

Rand Corporation, 36, 58
rapid deployment force, 84
readiness (combat), 80
Reagan, Ronald, 10, 23, 34, 44
Reagan, Ronald and Build-Down, 107, 109-110, 118
Reagan, Ronald, willingness to negotiate with USSR, 115-116

Reagan, Strategic program, 50
Rhodes, John, 87
Riegle, Donald, 70

S

SAC (Strategic Air Command), 8
SALT II (Strategic Arms Limitation Treaty), 23, 57, 104, 105, 109, 116
Schell, Jonathan, 95-96
Schmidt, Helmut, 13
Schroeder, Patricia, 54, 57
Scowcroft Commission, 62, 71, 73
Scowcroft Report, 69
second strike capability, 63
selective service, 39
SLBMS (sea-launched ballistic missiles), 3, 68
Social Democratic Party (German Federal Republic), 97
soft-target, 68
Sorenson, Theodore, 46
Speakes, Larry M., 110
Specter, Arlen, 67, 70, 72
SS-4, 12
SS-5, 12
SS-11,
SS-17, 63, 66
SS-18, 63, 66, 72, 73, 79
SS-19, 63, 66
SS-20, 12, 82, 96
SS-22, 13
SS-23, 13
SS-X-24, 72, 73
SSKP (single-shot-kill-probability), 63, 66
stability, 73
Stalin, 19
standing-start attack, 81

Star Wars, 61
START (Strategic Arms Reduction Talks), 67, 71, 107
Stennis, John, 86
Stevens, Ted, 42, 43, 70, 86, 88
Stockholm (Conference on Security and Disarmament), 23
Stockholm Conference, 116
strategic defense, 60
submarines, detection of, 68
Supreme Court, 33
survivability, 64-65, 113
survivability (MX), 57

T

Tank, M-1, 42
terror, balance of, 3
Test Ban, Limited Nuclear treaty, 20
tests, underground, 23
Thatcher, Margaret, 26
triad, strategic, 51
TRIDENT II, 7, 59, 66, 68
Trident missile, 25, 50, 59, 70
Trident, submarine, 50
troop reduction (NATO), 85-86
Tsongas, Paul, 61, 110
Turkey, 44

U

U-2, 20

V

verification, 61, 106
Vietnam, 31, 45
Vladivostok Agreement of 1974, 23, 115
vulnerability, 64

vulnerability (ICBM), 7
vulnerability (MX), 64, 70

W

war fighting, 68
war fighting doctrine, 58, 68

War Powers Act of 1973, 32, 33, 41, 46
Warsaw Pact (WTO), 13, 86
weapons, Soviet quality, 79
weapons, strategic, 3
Weinberger, Caspar, 27, 28
window of vulnerability, 73, 115

ABOUT THE AUTHORS

Werner J. Feld holds the rank of Distinguished Professor of Political Science at the University of New Orleans, where he has served since 1965. His academic career has been devoted to the study of U.S. policy in the international community. He has served as George C. Marshall Professor of Political Science at the College of Europe in Bruges, Belgium and at this writing is Fullbright Professor at the University of Innsbruck, Austria.

John K. Wildgen is Professor of Political Science at the University of New Orleans where he has taught since 1967. A former European Communities Fellow and NATO Fellow, he has been a pioneer in applying American quantitative methods to the study of comparative politics and foreign policy.

The two are long-time collaborators in the study of international cooperation, having co-authored *Domestic Political Realities and European Unification* (Boulder, Colorado: Westview Press, 1976). They have also worked in tandem in the study of international conflict. Their first joint study in this field was *NATO and the Atlantic Defense: Perceptions and Illusions* (New York: Praeger, 1982).

This book grows out of the same general interests that spurred the other works but differs in focus and in methodology. Rather than focusing on mass opinion viewed through statistics, it concentrates on elite attitudes and philosophies viewed through the speeches, statements, debates, and writings of Senators and Representatives who have interested themselves in the problems of defense and the maintenance of peace.